Seven Soccer Skills

A Footballing Guide for Parents, Coaches and Young Players

An educational and coaching manual for boys and girls and all persons involved in the development of young football players

Seven Soccer Skills

A Footballing Guide for Parents, Coaches and Young Players

Published by
Lagavara Publishing
This edition first published in 2018
ISBN 978-1-9999021-0-0
Copyright © Trevor McMullan, 2018

Photography: Françoise Caruana

Published by Lagavara Publishing, 19 Ashgrove Avenue, Naas, Co. Kildare, Republic of Ireland.
Book layout by Salient Print Management, Naas, Republic of Ireland.
Printed by W&G Baird Ltd., Caulside Drive, Antrim, Northern Ireland.

FOREST
STEWARDSHIP
FSC COUNCIL

This book has been printed on sustainable products from FSC managed forests.
"FSC" stands for Forest Stewardship Council, an organisation that works to promote the
practice of sustainable forestry worldwide.
The Forest Stewardship Council sets standards for forest products and independently certifies
that these standards have been met.

"*Seven Soccer Skills* is an exciting new book for all young football players. It encourages parents and guardians to play an active role in the early developmental stage of young players as they learn the football techniques required to become talented and skilful footballers.

Michael O'Neill

For many volunteers and qualified coaches, the text offers useful drills and practical pointers on how to run purposeful training sessions that are both enjoyable and constructed with safety in mind.

The author, Trevor McMullan, has used his wealth of experience, both as a coach and as a player, to provide a valuable resource of tips and information.

Seven Soccer Skills supports the ethos of the Irish Football Association's Youth Football Strategy, which strives to create a fun, safe and inclusive culture, thus inspiring a lifelong love of the game.

I highly recommend this book."

Michael O'Neill
International Football Manager

CONTENTS

Chapter		Page

FOREWORD

Football is a game which enriches the lives of millions of people around the world. It can be played enjoyably at any level, by boys and girls, young and not so young and by people with a range of disabilities. Players' enjoyment is enhanced by a greater understanding of the game and also by improving their technique and skill. Trevor McMullan's excellent book aims to provide a basis for young people, their parents and coaches to improve players' performance and get the maximum pleasure from their sport.

Trevor has a wealth of relevant experience in football, both as a senior player and as a highly qualified coach, which he brings to this book. It is presented in a very user-friendly way which is both encouraging and supportive. The book uses illustrations and diagrams to gain understanding, and there are useful references to the laws of the game, knowledge of which is essential for players, coaches and all involved in the game.

I hope the reader finds this book stimulating and encouraging and that it enhances young people's involvement in and enjoyment of this wonderful game.

David Ager, Child Safeguarding Tutor.
Former Referee Instructor and Assessor, Cornwall FA.
Author, *The Soccer Referee's Manual*.
Co-author, *Handbook of Football Club Management*.

INTRODUCTION

"Have fun, make new friends and learn the fundamental techniques and skills to become the best footballer that you can be."

For the young footballer, their parents or guardians and their coaches, the above statement summarises what the experience of this wonderful sport should be about and is the starting point for this book. Enjoy!

Seven Soccer Skills is written as a practical guide to provide children, parents and coaches with the information necessary to help a young footballer prepare for eleven-a-side football.

There are two main stages of development for young footballers aged five to twelve years old. The first stage is the "fun stage". For children aged around five to nine, the emphasis is on enjoyment built around athletic and football skills, as well as mini-games.

The second stage is the "learning to train stage", with the emphasis increasingly on learning to train and to practise, technical development and mini-games. This stage is for the approximate age range of nine to twelve.

Each topic covered in this book is directed at the players, parents, and coaches. In many cases, parents will also become coaches and get involved in a club once their child becomes a member.

Initially, children will probably be introduced to this book through their parents. The diagrams and illustrations will enable them to recognise some of the techniques and skills. Ideally, as they get older, they will start to read the book for themselves. By the age of eleven or twelve, when they progress to eleven-a-side football, they should be able to use it independently to develop a clear understanding and knowledge of how to play the game successfully.

At the bottom of some pages, there are questions on the laws of the game, under the title of *You're the Ref!* As a first introduction to these laws, they are intended to be fun as well as interesting and challenging. Many of the more complex laws of the game need only be explained to the players as they mature.

SETTING THE GOALPOSTS

Sympathetic coaches and encouraging parents are essential to help guide young players through the initial years of discovery, education and development. Children need to learn the game of football in a safe and friendly environment where they are taught, encouraged and challenged to become the best footballer they can be.

The amount of time that a child has in contact or playing with a football, wherever it may be, will have a significant bearing on their rate of development as a football player.

Playing football with their friends or on their own several times a week, combined with proper coaching, is more beneficial than playing a competitive match once a week in which they may not touch the ball all that often.

Spontaneous games with a small number of players therefore give the players better opportunities to practise the techniques and skills that they are taught in training and coaching sessions.

What is the role of the coach? It is to teach the young player the necessary football techniques and skills at the appropriate time in the player's development. Coaches encourage players and challenge them, and help them become confident and learn the game of football in a fun and safe environment. The focus at this stage should not be on results but on developing the footballing skills of the young player.

What is the role of the responsible parent of an aspiring young footballer? It should be to encourage, support and provide an atmosphere in which the player feels secure, confident and happy to play a sport which is enjoyed by many children the world over.

Young players should be urged to think and ask questions about the game, because football is primarily about making judgements and decisions. They should be encouraged to make these footballing decisions and to try new techniques and skills. Critically, they need to feel that they will be supported as they embrace the many emotions and challenges that come with learning new ideas.

This book will provide key information that players, parents and coaches can use to ensure that the critical foundation stages of a child's footballing life are both positive and fun-filled.

② LET'S MEET THE TEAM

This book hopes to help parents, coaches and players achieve a series of mutually complementary targets – the first and most important being to enjoy their engagement with this universal game.

THE ROLE OF PARENTS

1. Inspire and support your child to learn the various football techniques and skills.
2. Encourage your young person to make new friends.
3. Try to ensure that your child has fun, and share in the joy as a family.

THE ROLE OF COACHES

1. Teach the players the key football techniques and skills at the correct stage in their development.
2. Encourage the young players to have fun and make new friends.
3. Develop your coaching skills.

THE ROLE OF PLAYERS

1. Learn the fundamental football skills and techniques.
2. Develop athletic skills and become fit, healthy and confident individuals.
3. Make new friends and have fun.

Finally, to have an impartial viewpoint and to keep an eye on proceedings, let us not forget about the referees.

Referees play a significant role in football. They need to learn and understand the laws of the game, be fair in their decision making and keep themselves in good physical condition. It is also essential to referee games in a friendly manner and, where possible, to communicate with the players and encourage fair play.

3 WHERE TO START?

PARENTS

This should be an exciting time to get involved in football, and hopefully you cannot wait to get started! Like most things in life, joining a football club is not without its anxieties. The would-be young footballer might not be that confident around other children, nor have played much football at all. However, given time and some gentle encouragement and persuasion, these issues can be overcome.

It is natural that most parents will have concerns about their budding footballer. A sensible first step is to watch the potential club or local clubs in action. How well organised are they? What are the facilities like? Are the young footballers suitably supervised? How are the standards of behaviour? What are the attitudes of the coaches like? What are the relationships between coaches and players, as well as player to player? If you come away with a positive view, then it is time to visit the football club formally to meet the chairperson, coaches or relevant people and get a feel for the club and its ethos from their perspective.

Ask about their child protection policies and measures as well as the coaching structure. A progressive club will understand the importance of child protection policies and of continual improvement in coaching standards.

Enquire if it is possible to see a football coaching session with the relevant age group. The coaches should be friendly, the exercise should be purposeful, and the children should appear to be having fun.

Many children and parents have been put off sport by the attitude and conduct of a coach or manager, many of whom do not seem to know what they should be doing. By carrying out this research, it should be possible to ensure that this does not happen to your child.

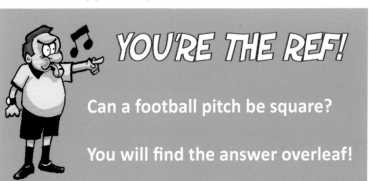

YOU'RE THE REF!

Can a football pitch be square?

You will find the answer overleaf!

In the real world, you may not have a great choice when it comes to selecting a club or its coaches. However, always remember that it is possible to learn the laws quite quickly, get on the coaching ladder and become an effective coach yourself!

Football is a simple game to play, and anybody with some time, commitment and enthusiasm can quickly become a talented football coach and an asset to any club.

Your national football association is a prime, initial source of information, and most experienced coaches are usually willing to give advice and help would-be coaches to get started. *(See pages 180 and 181 for a list of useful contacts.)*

YOU'RE THE REF!

Answer: No.
Law 1: The field of play must be rectangular.

COACH

When a coach is first introduced to a group of five- or six-year-olds, many of these children will have experience of kicking a football and playing with other small children. Some, however, will not.

It is likely to be stressful for a child who is attending football coaching for the first time. They may not know anyone and may have little experience of playing football. It is therefore essential to have a football available for every child so that they can start running around, kicking a football and having fun immediately. Ensure that the balls are of the correct size and air pressure.

Give praise and encouragement, and everybody will soon relax. A conscientious coach is continually assessing the confidence (and ability) of the players under his or her tutelage.

The first experience should be a positive one, so that all the young players will be eagerly looking forward to the next coaching session and meeting up with their new friends.

When possible, explain to the parents or guardian what the players are being taught, so that they can help the children perform the skill or technique at home. Have a chat with the parents at the end of the session and advise them how the children are to be dressed and equipped for training. This is described in detail in chapter 14 on "Proper Preparation".

An appropriate time to have a chat with the players about what you will be coaching is at the first drinks break, after the warm-up. Alternatively, you can have a brief discussion with the players before the coaching session starts, particularly if they develop a good habit of arriving early. This is beneficial especially if you are renting out the training area. Do not spend too much time talking, however, when the players can be playing football.

Tip 1. **Have a ball each for all the players and get started quickly.** Warming up and training are usually more enjoyable when the players have a football at their feet.

Tip 2. **Find out what the players know.** As you will only have limited contact with the players each week, it is useful to find out what they are learning and who is teaching them. It could be their parents, relatives, siblings, friends or other coaches at football camps or school. Indeed, having more than one coach helps to share the workload, considering that the vast majority of coaches are volunteers. Perhaps some parents are interested in helping you or even in learning to become a coach.

If so, an excellent way to introduce football coaching to new volunteers is to hold an introductory session for adults, where you demonstrate the principles of coaching in a fun and interactive manner. The exercise need not last any more than one hour, and hopefully you should have several enthusiasts who are interested in taking the first step to becoming a qualified coach.

If you or your club are not qualified or confident enough to take this on, you can contact your national football association *(see pages 180 and 181 for details).* They should be willing to help and put you in contact with the nearest qualified coach.

An example of a one-hour coaching session is described later in the book on page 166, which will be of particular benefit to any new football coach starting out in the game.

Asking players to demonstrate different skills and techniques is also helpful if you cannot do them yourself or if you are temporarily unable to. Children learn in many ways, and watching their friends or their peers perform skills can encourage and motivate them to do likewise.

Finally, remember that football can be enjoyed at all levels – resist the temptation to concentrate on the best players.

PLAYER

Learning to play the game of football should be a fun and pleasant experience, no matter what age you start. You should look forward to meeting your new friends at football training and practising your new skills at home as much as possible.

Learning the laws of the game can also help you understand how to play the game, but overall, just enjoy being taught by your coaches and playing and practising with your family, friends and teammates. While learning the game, you will develop your own unique playing style – enjoy having fun, being fit and healthy while making new friends!

Many of the fundamental skills and techniques in this book can be practised on your own, so try to find an area where you can practise regularly.

When you are learning a new skill, visualise or think of situations where you might use them in a game, and you will find that when you practise or play in a football match, you should be able to perform the skill more effectively.

As a parent or a coach, watching a young person develop confidence, knowledge and technical ability in their chosen field brings great satisfaction. Football is no different.

Young football players must be interested, enthusiastic and have confidence in those who are teaching them. They learn by listening, observing and experiencing. The more the players know what they can do, the more they will practise and the better footballers they will become. There are many ways to help a child build confidence, and gaining knowledge is one of them.

Football is a straightforward game to play. It is also easy to learn the fundamental laws of the game. The only law that causes any difficulty is the offside law, explained briefly on page 178. This law is not applicable in games with small numbers. Most players will know or have some understanding of the law by the time they begin to play eleven-a-side football at the age of eleven or twelve.

The Laws of the Game, produced by the International Football Association Board, can be downloaded from the Fédération Internationale de Football Association (FIFA) website www.fifa.com. As an option, the laws are also available in booklet form, usually for a small fee, from your country's football association. This booklet is a helpful means of becoming more familiar with the laws of the game.

In young footballers' formative years, knowledge can improve their confidence, as they will have the answers to some of the many questions they encounter in learning the game. Confidence in football is essential. Even at the highest level of football, lack of confidence is a major reason for a player's loss of form.

Participating in different sports and learning new skills will help young players develop as athletes and also boost their self-belief and confidence.

The information presented under the headings "Seven Techniques & Skills" and "Outside the Box" is designed to provide guidance for parents, coaches and players during this exciting developmental stage in a young footballer's life.

PARENTS

Most of the early years will be spent having fun and watching your child go from kicking their first football to joining their first team. Try to create an area at home where they can practise when on their own. They do not need a vast amount of space, as many of the techniques and skills can be learnt in an area of less than five metres square.

Playing with a small, light football is imperative in their early years. You can never have too many footballs.

Always try to say "Yes" if you are asked to play football. Easier said than done, I know! Most of the time, however, children just need a few minutes of your time to be satisfied. As a result, you will build a stronger relationship with them, and they will develop a more positive outlook on the game of football.

If your child is part of a team, always ask the coach and the young player what is being taught. Encourage the child to try to explain and demonstrate the skill when practising at home.

With the aid of this book, in particular the sections on the role of the coach and the role of the player, it should be possible to monitor and understand what your young footballer is being taught. If he or she is having fun, learning the fundamental football techniques and skills, and making new friends, then you are all on the right path.

COACH

You are a very important person in the education of the emerging football player. Be enthusiastic, have integrity, set high standards and be patient. Develop a friendly coaching style, have good football knowledge, understand how children learn, and aim to instil confidence in them. Help them develop their sporting and social skills, and if that is not enough, have the ability to inspire. No pressure, then! Always remember that you should have fun too.

Encourage the players to be considerate of others. Teach this by personal example, and help them to make as many friends as possible.

If you can, aim to upgrade your coaching qualifications. Education is a lifelong process, and coaching is one facet of training, so aim to improve your football knowledge and learning.

Finally, be proud of the fact that you are providing young players with the opportunity to participate in and enjoy this fantastic game. Marino Branch
Brainse Marino
Tel. 8336297

PLAYER

In the early years of your football development, the game is learnt from family, friends and football coaches. As you get older, you will read more about the game and its laws.

Play football to enjoy the game. If you join a team, have fun with your teammates and understand that each player has a part to play.

Do not be too influenced by the physical size and strength of your opponents or teammates, as it is often more important to have good mental abilities. To achieve this, practise ball games, either on your own or with your friends, which require your brain to make challenging decisions. For example, pass a football against a wall, and after a few passes try to control the ball and make a return pass with your eyes closed. To improve, concentrate and visualise where and when the ball will arrive at your foot.

Another game involves getting a friend to throw a ball at you. Once the ball is thrown, he or she shouts which hand you have to use to catch the ball. Respond by stepping out with the opposite foot before catching the ball. Practices like these will help your brain make new connections, increase your reaction speed and improve your concentration and confidence.

Balance, coordination, timing, concentration, and awareness of space are some terms used in the game of football. All are connected with the mental aspect of the game.

Improve your balance and strength by standing on one foot for, say, 30 seconds and then repeat with the other leg. Now, repeat the exercise with your eyes closed and notice how much harder it is. Practise this exercise. With added concentration, you will notice the improvement in your balance and strength.

These exercises should be challenging, enjoyable and part of your overall learning experience. Have as much fun as possible, and enjoy the process of learning the necessary footballing techniques and skills.

5 SEVEN TECHNIQUES & SKILLS

The seven techniques and skills in football are:

1. Passing
2. Dribbling
3. Shooting
4. Controlling
5. Heading
6. Goalkeeping
7. Tackling

PARENTS

Even with little or no knowledge of the game, the basic laws of football and the seven techniques and skills above can be quickly learnt and taught to your child. It is essential to play with your child, encourage and support them, and have fun with them as they go through the various stages of learning and development. It is possible to help a young player become a superb footballer through the purposeful practice of, and experimentation with, the various footballing techniques and skills.

COACH

A coach has an important role in helping a young footballer learn, understand and enjoy the game of football. The main objective for the coach is to teach the children the techniques and skills required to become all-round footballers. This can be achieved by allowing the developing player to learn and experience all the different positions in football.

While some players, at a young age, will show certain promise in a particular position, we must be aware that children develop at different rates during their early years, both physically and mentally. It would therefore be remiss of us as coaches if we overlooked a basic skill set at a critical time in a player's development.

A common question that people ask a young footballer is, "What position do you play?" How uplifting it would be if the player responds by saying that they are learning all the skills of a footballer and playing in different positions.

Dribbling the ball past them, effortlessly, you flick the ball up in the air and shoot with an overhead kick. In goals, there is a famous goalkeeper, but the shot is unstoppable and you have scored a brilliant goal!

If you remember your short story, it will be much easier to think of the necessary techniques to practise.

However, just as important as knowing what to learn is having the desire and determination to learn. You must have an interest and a real willingness to participate. Understand, from an early age, that enthusiasm, determination and dedication are three of the most important attributes you need to have to become a competent footballer.

PASSING

There are four main principles of passing:

1. Accuracy
2. Weight of pass
3. Timing
4. Disguise

PARENTS

In their early years, children will run around and chase after the ball, so getting them just to enjoy kicking a football is a good starting point. Gradually, however, we have to introduce the concept of passing a ball rather than kicking it. By learning the four principles of passing, it is possible to help your child become a confident and competent passer of the ball.

Using a rebound surface, such as a wall, is one way to encourage a young player to improve their passing technique. The wall will bounce the ball back to the player, thus allowing the practice to continue. This is both a fun and helpful way to enhance the skill of passing the ball.

COACH

Teaching a new technique or skill should be carried out at the start of a coaching session, after the players have warmed up and concentration levels are at their highest and not affected by fatigue. Young players learn and (unfortunately) forget easily. It is therefore necessary to repeat and hone these skills and techniques constantly if they are to become second nature.

Teaching a player to pass a ball accurately is one of the easiest and most enjoyable roles in football. The inside of the foot is the widest part of the foot, and therefore it is where most contact can be made with the football. Consequently, using the inside of the foot when passing makes it easier to be more accurate.

For a coach, choice of words can be very important in educating a young player. For example, when the word "pass" is used, the emphasis is on a more deliberate action compared to "kick". If the emphasis is on passing the ball rather than kicking it, developing players will become more conscious of their actions.

It can also be a useful idea to use the word "play" to begin exercises or to restart play in mini-games and practice matches. When the players play in competitive or organised games, they will often hear the referee telling them to "play on" when the referee plays advantage or thinks no foul has been committed. We want the players to have a positive and quick response when they hear these words.

To help encourage a player to pass rather than kick the ball, introduce a condition into mini-games so that a player has sufficient time to control a ball,

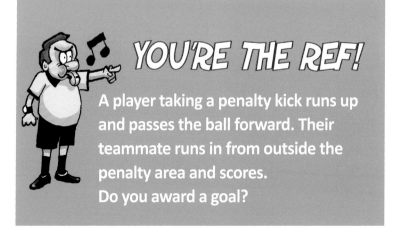

YOU'RE THE REF!

A player taking a penalty kick runs up and passes the ball forward. Their teammate runs in from outside the penalty area and scores.
Do you award a goal?

look up to see a teammate, make a successful pass and not be tackled. To do this, stipulate that the player receiving the pass cannot be tackled for, say, three seconds. This will give the player just enough time to have a quick look and make a pass without being tackled and losing possession of the ball. It will also encourage more successful passing and will help speed up the learning process.

We do not want young players to kick the ball away aimlessly because they are not confident enough to control the ball and make a successful pass to a teammate.

Encouraging the players to make their own decisions and to experience the outcome is much more important and effective than telling them what to do. Players must be supported to make decisions quickly and not to worry about mistakes, which are inevitable and a valuable part of the

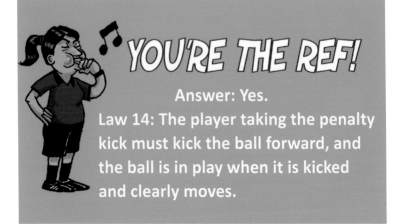

YOU'RE THE REF!

Answer: Yes.
Law 14: The player taking the penalty kick must kick the ball forward, and the ball is in play when it is kicked and clearly moves.

learning experience. Here, the role of the coach is to help the young player to be aware of any recurring problems so that, together, coach and player can resolve them.

When coaching in a small-sided game, it is more beneficial to ask a player if they can see someone to pass to, rather than to tell them what to do. This kind of question will prompt the player to look up and find a team member to whom they can pass the ball.

There are many exercises and drills that will help teach passing the ball. Here are three simple, enjoyable drills that can be used by any age group.

The maximum number of players needed at any one stage in the following exercises is three. Keeping the setup as simple as possible will help the players to repeat the exercise at home or in the park with their friends.

Exercise 1. The basic objective in the first exercise below is for the players to pass the ball through the red cones. The two main passing principles are accuracy and weight of pass. Each area or grid, as

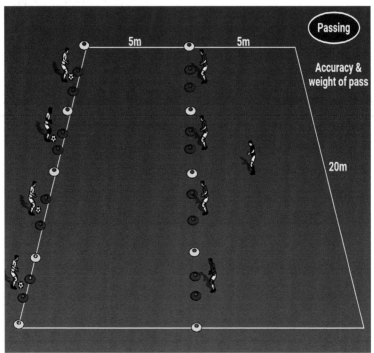

indicated by the yellow cones, is approximately five metres square, and the red cones act as goals. The players stand behind the goals and attempt to pass the ball through the red cones.

With the youngest age group, adjust the length of the area to make it slightly smaller and increase the size of the goals. The larger the goals, the more success each player will experience and the greater their enjoyment! The significance of success and enjoyment cannot be overstated. They are critical in nurturing a positive attitude in the young player and will facilitate their ongoing development.

Here are a few tips to help in the running of the exercise.

1. Choose an area where the players do not have to run far if they lose control of the ball.
2. If they lose control of the ball, teach them not to run into another player's area to retrieve it.
3. Regularly move one line along so that the players play with different teammates.
4. Ensure the players pass the ball with both the left and right foot.
5. As accuracy improves, reduce the size of the goals or increase the length of the grid.
6. Teach the players how to concentrate, by setting a target of a certain number of goals in a specified time frame (or turn it into a competition – first to ten completed goals).

Introduce coaching points associated with passing.

Remind the players to:

- keep their heads up;
- make eye contact with their playing partner;
- keep their eye on the ball when making their pass;
- keep their knee over the ball if the aim is to pass the ball low or on the ground.
- call their teammate's name when they want to receive a pass;
- take one touch to control the ball and one touch to pass.

This final point is not always possible or practical but usually can be best achieved by controlling the ball with the inside of the foot. The ball should be correctly positioned for the player to pass the ball back to their teammate using only one more touch. This forces the player to concentrate on a good first touch of the ball.

It is imperative to ask the players why they do certain things and to encourage lots of answers, whether or not the players answer correctly.

In any teaching, the following is central to effective learning:

The quality of the questions will determine the quality of the answers.

For this reason, pre-prepared questions are more liable to coax the desired response. Players working things out for themselves is always much more useful than giving them the answers.

Exercise 2. The second exercise *(see diagram overleaf)* is another fun way to practise passing the ball with the perfect weight: not too hard or too soft. Again it can be done with any age group. One player can do this on their own, but it is much more enjoyable with several players.

When coaching several players, it is vital to get as many of them as possible playing with a football as much as possible. Therefore, when setting up exercises, it is usually much better to have more columns of players than rows of players. For example, in this second exercise, there are four columns of two players instead of two columns of four. This way the players get much more practice with the football and therefore will learn more quickly. They will also be more likely to respond to your coaching tips.

YOU'RE THE REF!

A player plays a high pass down the touchline. The ball curls out over the touchline and back into play.
Do you allow play to continue?

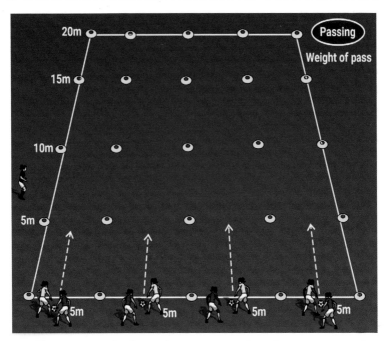

The aim of the above exercise is to pass the ball accurately and with perfect weight, out to the various target lines. Once the pass has been made, the player sprints after the football and retrieves

YOU'RE THE REF!

Answer: No.
Law 9: The ball is out of play when it has wholly passed over the goal line or touchline on the ground or in the air.

it, but only after it has passed the target line. The player then returns to the start as quickly as possible. If the ball does not reach the target line, then the player must repeat the exercise. Once the first player has returned to the starting line, the next teammate begins. It soon becomes clear to the player that if their pass is under-hit *(not kicked hard enough),* then they will be standing waiting for the ball to reach the target line.

Conversely, if the player hits the pass with too much weight *(kicked too hard),* then he or she will have to run much faster and further to retrieve the ball. However, it will soon become evident that it is better not to under-hit a pass, as this results in having to repeat the exercise. This is a valuable lesson for the player to learn because, in a match, if they make a firm but accurate pass to a teammate, then usually the teammate should be able to adjust and control that pass. However, if the pass is too weak or under-hit, an opponent is likely to intercept the ball. A skilled player will much rather receive a firmly struck pass, because they will have confidence in their ability to control the ball.

Many variations of this exercise can be introduced. For example, once the players have retrieved the ball after their initial pass, they can either dribble back, chip the ball back, or pass it to their teammate and sprint back.

as the ball reaches them. It will also help them learn about both the timing and weight of the pass.

If they pass the ball too soon, or with too much weight, there will be nobody at the other end to receive it. Pass the ball too late, or under-hit it, and the person at the other end will be standing waiting for the pass to reach them.

Introduce a competition to find out which team can make the most consecutive passes in a certain amount of time. Thirty to sixty seconds is sufficient. This exercise encourages the players to pass accurately with the correct weight and timing. The exercise should flow quickly and smoothly, and the team with the most consecutive passes wins.

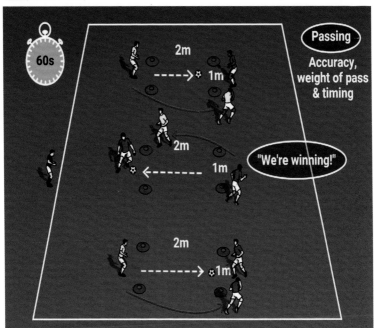

Again, the competitive element adds fun to the exercise.

The exercise can easily be adapted if it is necessary to add more players: simply increase the size of the grid. Other conditions can be added to make this more challenging; for example, using the right or left foot only, or restricting the players to one or two touches. Running anti-clockwise will encourage a right-footed pass, and clockwise, a left-footed pass.

If the players are instructed to take two touches of the ball, then they will have to concentrate, as their first touch must set the ball up correctly for them to make an accurate, precisely weighted return pass with their second touch. The first touch must not allow the ball to stay too close to their foot, where they cannot get the power they need to make the appropriate pass. Nor must it move the

YOU'RE THE REF!

At kick-off, a player passes the ball forward to their teammate, who is standing in the opposing half.
Do you allow play to continue?

ball too far away, where they have to run after it in order to make the pass. Taking at least two touches is much more realistic for younger age groups, as most children will need to control the ball first before they can make an accurate pass.

A significant factor in passing is disguise. This is important but not as critical as accuracy, weight of pass and timing. By the time the players have perfected these first three principles, they will have most likely figured out how to disguise a pass and fool an opponent.

Disguising a pass is trying to get an opponent to believe a pass is going in a specific direction but then sending it in a direction that the opponent had not expected.

Once the players understand how to pass correctly and with confidence, it is much easier to teach them how to create space and make good angles when receiving and making a pass.

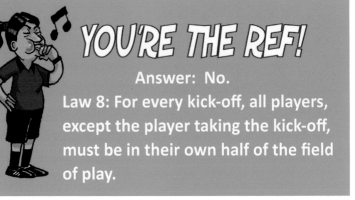

YOU'RE THE REF!

Answer: No.

Law 8: For every kick-off, all players, except the player taking the kick-off, must be in their own half of the field of play.

PLAYER

Passing the ball is one of the most important techniques in football. To perfect the art of passing, first learn the basic principles and then practise them. It is easy to practise alone: all you need is a solid surface to bounce the ball against so that it comes back.

Is the ball doing what you want it to do, and if not, why not? Visualise the pass by thinking of which part of the foot to use, how hard to strike the ball, where the ball should go and which part of the ball to hit. To keep the ball on the ground, keep the knee over the ball. To send the ball into the air, lean back and kick the bottom part of the ball. Watch to see if the ball does exactly what was intended, and make adjustments if it does not.

Remember to practise with both feet and concentrate mainly on short passes of about five to ten metres. If young players can consistently pass accurately over this distance, then as they get older and physically stronger, they will be able to pass the ball much further with the same accuracy.

Tip. **If an opponent is close and you are trying to make a short pass, use an "air pass".** A ground pass close to the opposing player could easily be intercepted by an outstretched leg. But if the ball is chipped slightly off the ground between the opponent's outstretched foot and knee, then it is extremely difficult for them to intercept the pass.

This is an advanced skill and can be used in tight spaces and against skilled opponents.

The following are some other skills and footballing terms which are associated with passing the ball, but they are used less often and are more unpredictable in their outcome.

Toe-Poke. The "toe-poke" is literally to poke or prod the ball with the toe of the boot. It is mostly used to kick the ball away quickly if tackling or making a quick pass or shot and there is no other option. There is less accuracy with this type of pass or shot, as there is little surface area contact between the  foot and the ball. The toe-poke is an instinctive action and is used mostly in haste. However, it can catch opponents by surprise and is a useful skill to learn and practise.

Rabona. This is a difficult skill and very seldom used in a game. It is, however, an impressive skill to master. If the ball is on the outside of the standing foot, bring the opposite leg around the back of this leg and kick down and under the ball.

Back-Heel. This is simply kicking the ball with the heel of the foot and can be used to catch opponents by surprise.

There are two ways to back-heel the ball. The first is when the ball is on the outside of the foot. Bring the other leg or non-standing leg across the front of the ball and use the heel to kick the ball backwards.

The second way to back-heel is with the heel of the foot which is in front of the ball. In order for the ball to go backwards in a straight line, the ball must be struck evenly with the heel of the foot.

Spin. Practising and experimenting are essential to learn about spin. Practise spinning a ball with the hands and let it drop to the ground to see the effect of different types of spin. Rotate the ball backwards for back-spin, forwards for

top-spin and sideways for side-spin. Now use your foot and observe the ball rotation as you experiment. Creating back-spin on the ball, for example, can help to keep the ball close to the player when playing "keepie uppies", as the ball will always spin towards the player and not away from them.

If the ball is on the ground, kicking down and underneath it can force the ball to rise and spin backwards. When the ball lands, the spin makes it stay close to the spot where it landed. This is an excellent skill to use if attempting to play a ball over the opposing defence for a teammate to run on to, particularly if space is restricted.

Top-spin is when the ball spins forward. If the ball hits the ground with top-spin, it will continue to travel forwards quickly from the spot where it landed. *(See image below.)*

Side-spin will force the ball to spin off to the side when it hits the ground. Weather and pitch conditions can also be significant, so it is essential to practise and experiment as much as possible.

DRIBBLING

7

PARENTS

Dribbling with a football is a fun technique to learn. It is different from running with the ball in that the ball must be kept close to the foot. Running with the ball usually occurs when there is free space to run into, and close control of the ball is not as important as speed. Here the head can be up to see what is happening in front of and around the player.

Dribbling is more precise and requires excellent balance and close control of the ball. Usually the head is down, with the eyes fixed on the ball and on the opponent nearby.

Dribbling is something that parents can quickly teach or help their child with. Not much space is needed. If you start with a slightly soft ball, it will stay closer to the foot and make it much easier to keep under control. Dribbling around objects can add to the fun, as all the family can join in. As children get more confident and competent, encourage them to use both feet.

COACH

Coaching children how to dribble with a ball correctly can require some time and patience. When first asked to dribble with the ball, young players will usually concentrate on running fast, where the ball will not be under control, or the more cautious will move very slowly, and the ball hardly leaves their foot.

An excellent way to teach dribbling is to use the concept of one step, one touch. This means that for every step taken, there is a touch of the ball. This is particularly important when dribbling up to an opponent. Having the ball close to the feet will prevent an opponent from taking the ball and offers the best chance of successfully dribbling past them. Having close control of the ball will also facilitate changes of direction and increase the likelihood of maintaining possession.

When teaching dribbling, it is imperative to focus initially on technique rather than speed. The tendency is for the player to run too fast and lose control of the ball, much to their dissatisfaction. *(See some examples below.)*

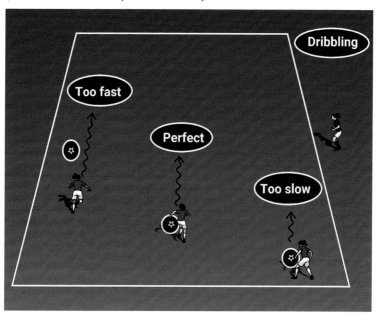

Visualisation, or forming a mental image, can help children learn a technique or skill more quickly and is useful in learning to dribble. To help the

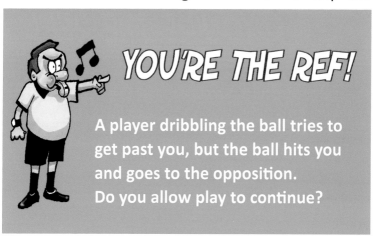

players understand this, start without the ball and pretend to dribble around a few cones. Stress the concept of one step, one touch. Bend the knee over the ball and pretend to touch the ball forward using the inside and outside of the foot.

Ask the players to repeat this, and it will be evident that they still tend to run too quickly. Only when they have slowed down sufficiently should the ball be introduced. There is little point in dribbling fast with no control.

Players should practise with both feet, and after the ball has been introduced, everyone should see the immediate improvement, with the ball staying close to the foot.

This skill can be taken to the next level by asking the players to dribble around in a confined area, where they will have limited space and have to

YOU'RE THE REF!

Answer: Yes.

Law 9: Provided that the ball has not wholly passed over the goal line or touchline, the ball is in play when it rebounds off a match official, goalpost, crossbar or corner flagpost and remains in the field of play.

avoid each other. This should be fun, so allow them to use whatever foot they want and enjoy themselves. As always, instructions should be given in a clear, friendly, enthusiastic and encouraging manner.

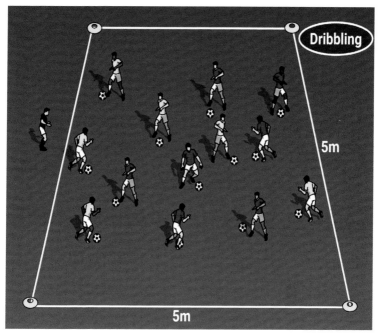

Again, emphasise the importance of taking one touch of the ball for every step taken. Ask the players the reasons they should do this. Hopefully, they will all be able to explain that if they do not keep the ball under control and close to their foot, then an opponent will take the ball from them.

Calling out "Stop!" will encourage the players to keep the ball close to their feet, as they do not want to be the last person to get the ball under control and stop. Help them learn to keep their heads up by using nonverbal signals to stop, play, etc., so that they have to be looking up and around to see these signals being used.

Remind the players, when dribbling, to keep their knee over the ball and to touch the ball forward with the outside and top of their foot in order to move at optimum speed. This is most important when they want to move quickly in a specific direction.

Once they are all dribbling correctly, remind the players of the importance of looking up and around. Potentially, this will allow them to:

- see where their teammates are to pass to;
- see where their opponents are;
- see where the goals are.

Once the players are dribbling with the ball under constant control, taking one touch for every step, able to stop consistently on command, keeping their heads up and using both feet, then they have mastered the basics, and it is time to add feinting, change of pace, obstacles and turns.

Exercise 1. The following exercise is a simple example where dribbling can be taught to many players in a safe and controlled manner. *(See overleaf.)* This structured exercise allows a coach to see clearly how the players are learning and progressing. Two or three rows of players wearing different-coloured bibs can make it easier to give clear and concise instructions. For example, if the yellows are to dribble to the ten-metre line using their right foot, you can simply say, "Yellows. Right foot dribble. Ten metres. Play!" This kind of instruction saves time, and the players understand precisely what they have to do.

Remember, keeping instructions clear and concise means there is more time to be spent demonstrating, practising and playing. The colour of the cones can also be changed to mark the various distances if it makes it easier for a younger age group.

YOU'RE THE REF!

A player dribbling the ball towards their opponent's penalty area is tripped outside the penalty area but falls inside the penalty area.
Do you award a penalty?

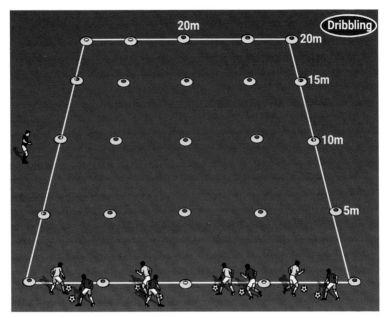

It is also essential to give the players some responsibility and encourage them to make their own decisions. For example, ask the yellow team to dribble up to the fifteen-metre line, and tell the red team they can begin once the yellow team

YOU'RE THE REF!

Answer: No.
Law 13: In this instance, the free kick is taken from the place where the offence occurred, which was outside the penalty area.

has safely passed the five-metre line. This strategy means that all the players are dribbling at the same time, and you can observe and give commands to test their dribbling ability and ball control.

The same exercise is beneficial when adding new skills. Simply place some extra cones or markers for the players to dribble through using the inside and outside of both feet. Everybody enjoys these exercises no matter what their age.

Sometimes when dribbling towards an opponent, the best way to get past is by playing a "one-two" with a teammate. This is also known as a wall pass. This passing movement is where a player passes to a teammate and continues running. The teammate then passes the ball back into the path of the first

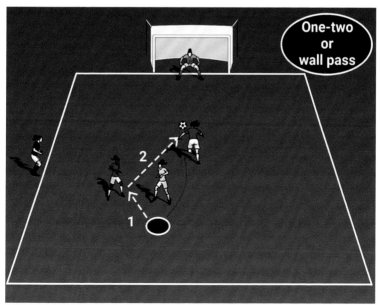

Another simple but useful trick is to move your foot over the ball as if you were going to back-heel it – but this is only a feint before you continue running. The more convincingly these feints are executed, the more success they will bring. In using these feints successfully, the player is controlling the opponent.

It is also possible to trick an opponent by pretending to pass the ball in a certain direction. To do so, pretend to make the pass with the inside of the foot but then roll your foot onto the top of the ball. Quickly stop the movement and drag the ball back with the sole of the foot and move off in a different direction.

Stepover. One of the most effective skills to learn for dribbling is the stepover. This is another useful method of making the opponent react in the manner you want. When confronted by an opponent, move the leg over the ball and move the body to create the impression of going in that direction. If the opponent then proceeds to cover this, simply go the other way. The ball must remain close to the feet until the opponent begins

to move in the desired direction. Then go past by pushing the ball away with the outside of the non-standing foot. The stepover must be believable, and sometimes more than one may be required to

YOU'RE THE REF!

A goalkeeper catches the ball in their penalty area. They then dribble the ball out to the edge of the penalty area and handle the ball again. Is this allowed?

bring success. It is essential to practise with both feet so that your opponent will not easily anticipate your next move. Once this skill is mastered, it will prove extremely useful!

Dragback. This is simply using the sole of the foot to drag or pull the ball backwards. The player can do this to attempt to move past an opponent, to shield and protect the ball, or to change direction.

If an opposing player tries to tackle and gain possession of the ball, simply pull the ball back with the sole of the foot and move quickly away.

♪ *YOU'RE THE REF!*

Answer: No.
Law 12: An indirect free kick is awarded if a goalkeeper, inside their penalty area, touches the ball with the hands after releasing it and before it has touched another player.

Another way to drag the ball back is to put one's foot over the ball and pull it back between the legs with the inside of the foot *(see picture A).* It is then possible to choose which foot to move off on *(see picture B).*

Other ways to change direction with the ball are to use the inside and outside of the foot. Simply put the foot over the ball, and using the inside or outside of the foot, move away with the ball in another direction *(see pictures below).*

Nutmeg. The nutmeg is where one player passes the ball between another player's legs and runs around the unfortunate opponent. It is usually seen as an accomplished skill when performed deliberately. This is a fun skill to learn when players are small, as it generates brilliant fun and laughter.

When the opportunity presents itself, it is also an efficient way to get past an opponent. Everybody enjoys doing this skill, and everybody hates getting nutmegged!

Shield. This is the ability to put one's body between the ball and the opponent to stop them getting to the ball. The laws of the game state that shielding the ball is permitted, provided that "the ball is kept within playing distance, and the player does not hold off the opponent with his or her arms or body".

The most effective way of shielding the ball is to keep control of the ball with the foot which is furthest away from the opponent, but be prepared to move as the opponent tries to get the ball. Shielding the ball usually only happens for a few seconds at a time but is a vital skill to  master, no matter where you play on the football pitch.

8

SHOOTING

PARENTS

Most small children enjoy kicking a ball and scoring a goal, so learning to shoot should be fun and exciting. Shooting usually requires a little bit of space, and this is not always possible at home. However, if a small set of goals is available, this can help a child revel in scoring a goal.

Tip. **Initially, let the young player shoot from close to the goal, as this will foster accuracy and result in plenty of goals**. It is much easier to teach any skill when the players are experiencing success.

At first, most young players will kick the ball with their toes, but as they get older, they can be taught how to shoot by striking the ball with the instep and the inside and outside of the foot.

Using a light football will help the player observe and learn how the ball moves in flight, depending on which part of the ball they kick, how hard they kick it and which part of the foot they kick it with.

COACH

It can be a helpful idea to allow juniors to practise shooting into goals with no goalkeepers. This way the players will get a great feeling when they shoot and score a goal – no matter how weak the shot actually is! Playing without a goalkeeper can speed up a shooting exercise. Players get more chances to shoot, and there are plenty of goals and happy faces.

Award two goals for every shot that goes into the corners of the goal. This way the players will quickly learn that the best chance of scoring is to aim for the corners of the goal, as these are the hardest places for a goalkeeper to cover.

YOU'RE THE REF!

Can a player score directly from a kick-off?

By starting shooting practice using stationary footballs, the youngsters will enjoy much more success. It will also be easier to teach the players to keep their eye on the ball and kick right through it to generate the most power.

Once the players understand how to shoot and where to shoot, you can move on to shooting when the ball is rolling. This is a much harder skill and requires a lot of practice.

Shooting practice is always exciting, especially if the players are scoring with plenty of shots. Many shooting practices have one goalkeeper and everybody taking a shot at the unfortunate person. However, this tends to become tedious very quickly for the outfield players, especially if they are only getting one shot every two or three minutes.

An alternative is to line up all the players in a row facing the goal with a ball each. No goalkeeper

YOU'RE THE REF!

Answer: Yes.
Law 8: A goal may be scored directly against the opponents from the kick-off.

is required. Players take a shot quickly one after the other, and nobody retrieves their ball until each player has had a shot. This way nobody gets hurt by being hit with a ball, and it is fun running to get a ball to line up to take another shot. The players then move along one position so they take their next shot from a different angle and also, eventually, with their other foot.

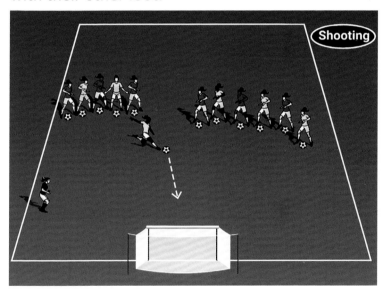

This exercise can be used to practise shooting when the ball is stationary and when it is moving. You can also vary the activity by crossing the ball so that the players are running onto the ball and shooting and scoring goals with different parts of the foot or body.

A goalkeeper can be used when coaching shooting in pairs. One player shoots and the other

one tries to score from a rebound if the goalkeeper saves the ball or if it hits the goalposts or crossbar.

PLAYER

Shooting can be practised alone by striking a stationary ball against a wall or other rebound surface. Put marks on the wall to encourage greater accuracy, and vary the distance to see how the ball dips and curls depending on how, where and how hard it is struck.

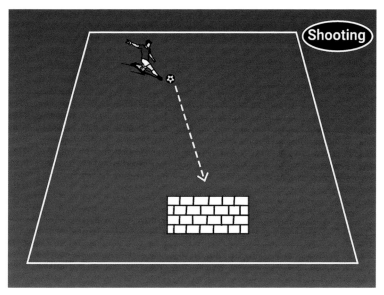

Learn how to make the shot stay on the ground by keeping the knee over the ball. Lean back and kick underneath the ball if raising it is the aim.

YOU'RE THE REF!

You award a team an indirect free kick outside their opponent's penalty area. A player takes the free kick, and the ball goes directly into the goal. Do you award a goal?

Remember to ask, "Is the ball doing what I want it to do? If not, why not?" Remember also to practise with both feet and then progress to striking a moving ball, which is more difficult. By practising regularly, and with expert coaching, the developing player will soon learn how to shoot accurately using proper technique.

As a young player, do not be concerned about getting power into the shot, as this will come with age and maturity. There are many ways to score a goal using the feet. Learning how to make the ball do what you want will increase the chances of scoring a goal.

There are some other football techniques and skills which can be learnt when shooting at goal, with or without a goalkeeper.

Volley. A volley is a method of kicking or passing the ball when it is in the air. The two main types of

YOU'RE THE REF!

Answer: No.
Law 13: If an indirect free kick is kicked directly into the opponents' goal, a goal kick is awarded.

volleys are a volley on the laces and a side-foot volley. The technique itself is not difficult to learn, but the skill is in learning to control the resulting trajectory of the ball.

Below are two examples of volleying the ball using the laces of the boot, first from the front and then from the side.

One outcome when volleying is for the ball to rise into the air. To learn to keep it low to the ground, point the toes downwards and try to get the knee over the ball. This applies when the ball comes both from the front and from the side. There are different body positions to learn, depending upon where the ball is coming from and whether the player is defending or attacking.

The same principles apply to the side-foot volley. In this example, using the inside of the foot affords the best opportunity to control the ball in the desired manner. Getting in line with the flight of the ball, coupled with keeping an eye on the ball, gives the player the best chance to execute the pass successfully.

Half Volley. A half volley is a method of kicking or passing the ball as it comes down from the air and bounces up from the ground. It is quite a difficult skill to control the ball as it leaves the foot. Again, it is essential to ensure that the knee is over the ball as much as possible, if the aim is to keep the ball flight low.

Overhead Kick. This technique is sometimes known as the bicycle kick. It is a difficult skill to perform but one that all young players want to try.

One way to learn is to throw the ball into the air, raise your foot as high as possible and, as the ball is dropping, try to hook the ball over your shoulder. This helps with timing, as the aim is to connect with the ball at the highest point of the kick.

If the player falls backwards, it is vital to learn to land correctly. Begin to work on learning the bicycle kick by selecting a soft surface to avoid injury. Timing is all-important to successfully executing this skill. The most spectacular overhead kick is when the body leaves the ground entirely, and the player connects perfectly with the ball.

Chip. The chip is a way to get the ball off the ground and into the air. If using the instep of your foot, kick down and underneath the ball to make it rise. A chip is usually performed in a controlled and deliberate manner and can easily be executed by addressing the ball from directly behind or from an angle.

Lob. A lob is when the ball is sent in a high arc. It is an excellent way to get the ball to go over an opponent's head. For example, if the ball bounces

nearby, use the inside, outside or top of the foot to lift the ball over your opponent.

Curl. Curling is a way of bending the ball and occurs when the player strikes across the ball with the inside of the foot. Leaning back and kicking underneath the ball makes it rise into the air. Using a goalpost as a target allows the player to experiment to see how the ball curls depending on where it is hit, how hard it is struck and how much elevation is imparted. Make sure to practise in different weather conditions, as these will influence the trajectory of the curled ball.

One of the first things children will learn to do is to kick the ball from out of their hands and into the air. They will soon progress to kicking and catching the ball. Then they will be able to keep the ball up in the air a couple of times with their foot, and then many more times as they get older and stronger.

To perfect this skill of keeping the ball in the air, we need to ask ourselves, "Can we get the ball to do what we want it to do?" For example, to keep the ball in the air more than once, we need to employ the following skills:

1. Kicking the ball high enough to give us time to get our foot ready to kick it again – but not too high, as this will make the ball harder to control.

2. Kicking the ball accurately so it will stay close, enabling us to reach it with our foot and kick it again.

3. Kicking it with the top of the foot with our toes slightly curled towards us, so that the ball comes back to us and not away from us.

We can also visualise what we have to do and think about our accuracy and the weight of our kick before we do it. By doing all the above, we will "get the ball to do what we want it to do", and if we do not, we will be able to understand what went wrong and try to correct it.

COACH

Teaching children about control and controlling the ball on the ground and in the air should be fun.

There are many simple and enjoyable exercises that can be used to teach controlling the ball with the various parts of the body when the ball is in the air or on the ground.

The following exercises can be used for side-foot volleys, volleys on the laces, half volleys and many more skills. They are enjoyable, and it is simple to add your own ideas and change the size of the area if necessary.

Exercise 1. In this exercise *(see overleaf)*, player 1 throws the ball to position B. Player 2 moves quickly across to position B, where they control the ball in the air with their right foot before volleying it back into the hands of player 1. Player 1 then throws the ball to position C for player 2 to move swiftly across and repeat the skill using the left foot.

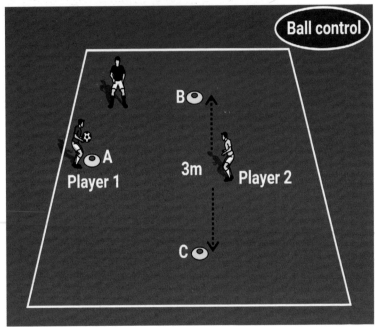

To practise controlling the ball on the ground, ask both players to take one touch to control the ball before passing it back. Vary the return pass by asking player 2 to pass the ball on the ground or to chip it into the arms of player 1. Various types of control can be added, such as thigh control, chest control or control with the inside and outside of the foot when the ball is in the air. Many of the skills are simple to practise individually using a rebound surface such as a wall, or with another player.

Exercise 2. Another enjoyable and useful exercise for ball control is as follows. Players 2, 3 and 4 have

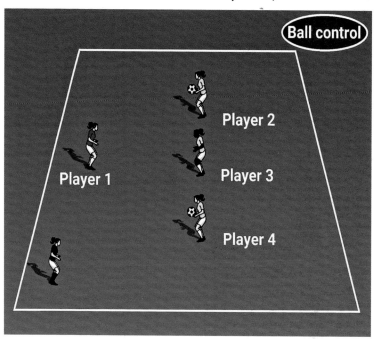

Ball control

Player 1

Player 2

Player 3

Player 4

two balls between them and stand approximately three metres away from player 1. This distance can be reduced for younger age groups. Holding the

YOU'RE THE REF!

What is the maximum time a goalkeeper can hold on to the ball once they have control of the ball in their hands?

ball in their hands, they throw the ball one at a time to player 1. In this example, player 1 then controls the ball on her thigh and volleys the ball back to the player who does not have a ball. Communication can be encouraged between the players, and a competitive element can be added by recording which player completes the most successful passes in a specific time period.

This exercise can be used for controlling and passing the ball on the ground, side-foot volleys, half volleys, volleys on the laces, chest control, control with the thigh and control with the head. Players change places regularly, and depending on the skill level, the tempo of the throws and the distance between the players can be adjusted. This exercise can be enjoyed by any age group and is simple to set up and control.

♪ YOU'RE THE REF!

Answer: Six seconds.
Law 12: An indirect free kick is awarded if a goalkeeper, inside their penalty area, controls the ball with the hands for more than six seconds before releasing it.

Exercise 3. In this next exercise, many players can practise ball control at the same time. For example, to practise thigh control, players in line A will throw the ball to their partner opposite, who then controls the ball on the thigh before passing the

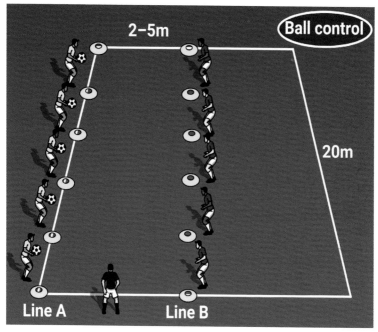

ball back. Many combinations are possible, such as right thigh control with a right foot pass, right thigh control with a left foot pass, and the same with the left thigh. Pass the ball back on the ground or in the air. Practise volleys, half volleys, headers and chest control in this safe and straightforward exercise.

Exercise 4. Progress to practising these skills while the players are running. In this exercise *(see overleaf)*, players in line B, who do not have the ball, move along the line to their right. They then receive a pass (or whatever technique or skill they are practising) from all of line A and eventually, by running around the blue cones, they will end up back at their starting positions. To practise with the

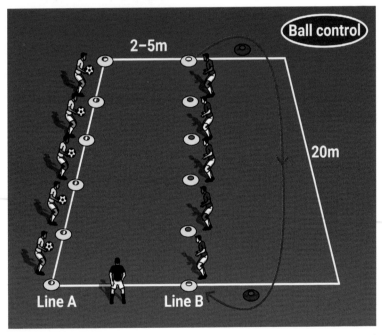

left foot, line B will simply turn left and run around the blue cones. Many of these skills are easy for the player to practise at home with a friend or two.

Players need to be taught how to control the ball on the ground with the outside of the foot in the same way as the inside of the foot. Teaching players to have a vision or an idea of what they want to do with the ball before controlling it will obviously influence their decision making.

PLAYER

Learning to control the ball on the ground and in the air – and all the different skills that go along with these techniques – should be challenging, fun and rewarding. To become a superb footballer, it is critical that the developing player perfects the ability to control an incoming ball with different parts of the body.

First, you must learn to control the ball on the ground. Using the inside of the foot is the easiest way to do this, as it is the widest part of the foot. The key elements of this skill are: getting in line with the flight or path of the ball as soon as possible, keeping your eye on the ball, withdrawing or relaxing the foot on impact with the ball, making contact with the middle of the ball, and keeping the knee slightly bent over the ball to help keep it on the ground.

To control the ball and then make a pass to a teammate, use a soft or relaxed touch with the foot so that the ball settles beside or in front of your feet, ready to be passed. This soft touch is achieved by relaxing or withdrawing your foot just as the ball hits it.

If your foot is not sufficiently relaxed on impact with the ball, then the ball will bounce away. On the other hand, if your foot is too relaxed, the ball will land or stay too close to your foot, and you will have to adjust your standing position to make the desired pass. This will take extra time and may allow an opponent to make a tackle.

If you know what you want the ball to do, then there is a much greater chance of completing a pass. Thinking like this will help you learn more quickly and work out solutions to get the outcome you want.

It is vital to practise with both feet to improve balance, leg strength and overall confidence. Excellent ball control is essential to become a skilled footballer.

The ball can also be controlled or trapped using the sole of the foot. This is a slightly harder way to control the ball, as the angle of the foot must be correct to trap the ball between the ground and the sole of the boot. This is, however, a useful skill to master because the ball will be instantly under control and the player should have more time to consider what to do with it.

When learning to control the ball in the air, just about every part of the body may be used – the foot,

YOU'RE THE REF!

The ball suddenly bursts just as a player controls the ball and scores a goal.
Do you award a goal?

thigh, stomach, chest and head. Controlling the ball in the air with the foot is similar to controlling the ball on the ground.

The few centimetres that the foot is lifted off the ground will allow the player to relax the foot and withdraw it downwards on impact with the ball. This can be achieved with either the side or the top of the foot. The side of the foot has the largest surface area and therefore delivers a much higher success rate.

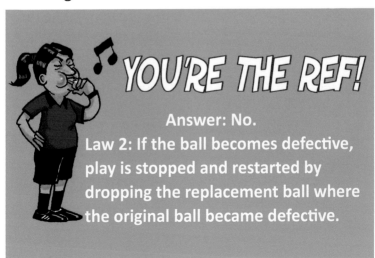

YOU'RE THE REF!

Answer: No.

Law 2: If the ball becomes defective, play is stopped and restarted by dropping the replacement ball where the original ball became defective.

Using the thigh to control the ball in the air is an important skill to learn. The thigh is a softer area of the body where it is easier to relax the muscles and soften the impact of the ball.

Using the inside and outside of the thigh can also help to control and direct the path of the ball. The front of the thigh is the part used most often to control the ball. To get the ball to drop to the foot, point the thigh downwards and relax the thigh muscles. To

get the ball to go up in the air, bend the leg and lift the knee for the thigh to make contact with the ball.

To practise thigh control, drop the ball onto the thigh and try to catch it. Usually, it will bounce away. Bending the leg and raising the knee will cause the ball to bounce upwards off the thigh, and with a little practice, the player will soon catch the ball each time.

The aim with thigh control is usually to soften the impact of the ball so that it drops to the ground ready for a pass. However, it is possible to use the thigh to make a short pass by tightening the thigh muscles and moving and pointing the thigh in the desired direction. Learning to control the ball in this way with both thighs is a valuable skill in football and is one of the best ways to control the ball as it comes down from the air.

Another way to control the ball in the air is with the body trap. Here the body is positioned so that when the ball bounces up off the ground, it will hit the stomach area. The body has to be bent over so that the ball immediately bounces down to the ground  ready to be played with the foot.

Obviously, the stomach is a soft part of the body, so the ball should not bounce too far away. This is an effective skill to have mastered, particularly when playing on a bumpy surface or if the ball bounces awkwardly in front of the player.

Controlling the ball with the chest and the head is more difficult, because both are harder surfaces and can sometimes be painful if the skill is not executed correctly. For chest control, puff out the chest just before impact with the ball, then the player will be  able to exhale and relax the chest when the ball makes contact.

To direct the ball to make a short pass, keep the chest puffed out and turn the body, if necessary, to guide the ball in the required direction.

When controlling the ball with the head in order to keep the ball near, withdraw the forehead just as it makes contact with the ball. Also, bend the knees

You can also help them learn by holding a ball a few inches from their forehead. The child can kneel and learn how to move their body towards the ball from their waist, making contact with the ball with the centre of the forehead. Progress to a standing position, and the player can learn how proper placement of the feet helps them to balance and position themselves to head the ball correctly.

COACH

Most children will have some experience of heading a ball — not all of it good! The first thing to teach young players is to head the ball with their forehead and to keep their eyes open. They should all have a light football and practise by first holding the ball in their hands and then bringing it into contact with their forehead while keeping their eyes open and mouth shut. They can then throw the ball into the air (not much more than head height to begin with) and experience the ball dropping and making contact with their forehead. The next stage is to see if the players can head the ball up in the air a couple of times, as this will show they have some degree of control of the ball – they are getting it to do what they want it to do. At this stage, there is no

need for the players to be jumping to head the ball.

You can teach the main points of heading by dividing the players into pairs, with one ball between two. Show them the ideal stance: one leg in front of the other, front foot pointing forward, and using the arms for balance. The head should be

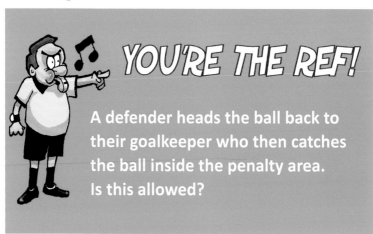

YOU'RE THE REF!

A defender heads the ball back to their goalkeeper who then catches the ball inside the penalty area.
Is this allowed?

up and move forward to meet the ball as it is *gently* thrown towards them. The objective is to head the ball accurately back into their partner's hands.

Once players understand the basics of heading a football, they should become more confident, and

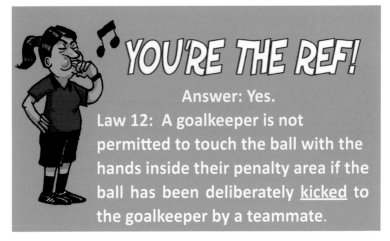

YOU'RE THE REF!

Answer: Yes.

Law 12: A goalkeeper is not permitted to touch the ball with the hands inside their penalty area if the ball has been deliberately <u>kicked</u> to the goalkeeper by a teammate.

it will be easier at a later stage to teach them about power, distance and jumping to head the ball.

Many young players will try to jump to head the ball even when they do not have to. It is more important to teach them about trying to watch the flight of the ball and to get into the right position from which to head the ball.

PLAYER

For the developing player, a valuable tip is to get in line with the flight of the ball as early as possible. This makes it easier to anticipate where the ball will land and to take up the best position to head the ball. Then hold that position so it is much harder for an opponent to get to the ball. The opponent will have to try to move you out of the way or be forced to jump much higher.

These tips make heading the ball easier to learn and should result in more confidence in heading the ball correctly and in the desired fashion. To add power to the header, arch the head back, bend the knees, and move the head forward to meet the ball.

Probably the toughest skill to learn in heading the ball is when having to jump for it. In this scenario, timing is crucial, as players usually need to be at the highest point of their jump when contacting the ball. Mastering this skill involves learning how to jump, how high to jump and when to jump.

A simple practice is to throw the ball gently into the air, then run and jump and try to head the ball at the highest point of the jump. Even if the proper connection with the ball is not made, under these circumstances it will not hurt. Continued practice will improve timing and technique.

Whatever position you play in a game or match, inevitably you will end up having to head a ball either defensively or offensively. The aim with defensive headers is to head the ball in a controlled

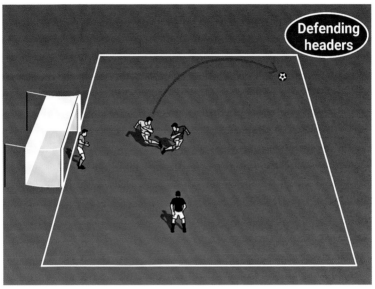

Defending headers

manner, accurately and with as much height and distance as possible, usually away from the centre of the pitch.

YOU'RE THE REF!

A player standing in an offside position heads the ball into their opponent's goal directly from a throw-in.
Do you award a goal?

Attacking headers are usually about accuracy and heading the ball downwards and, where possible, away from the goalkeeper. Heading the ball down towards the goal makes it much harder

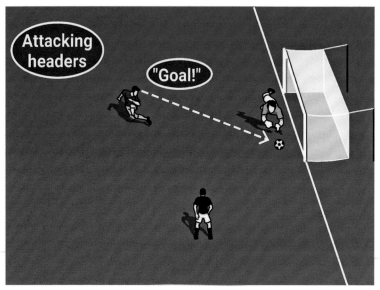

for a goalkeeper to reach and make a save. Learning to head the ball into the corners of the goal will ensure the best chance of scoring.

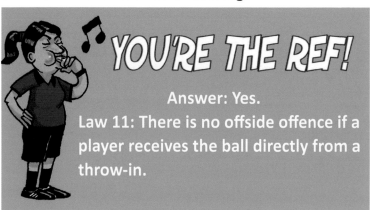

Tip. **When defending, always anticipate the ball coming to you or to the player you are marking.** If this player is taller than you, get in front of them and jump as high as possible. This should prevent your opponent from getting an easy header at goal.

Sometimes you may have to dive to head the ball, whether defensively or offensively. Concentrate on making contact with the ball with the centre of your forehead and heading it in the desired direction. It is essential to learn how to land correctly using your arms and chest.

Flicking the ball with the top of the head while moving your head backwards is a useful skill to learn, particularly in defence when you want to head the ball back to your goalkeeper. Learn also how to make glancing headers by using your forehead to make contact with the side of the ball to head it in the desired direction. Do not use the side of your head.

When practising jumping to head the ball, remember to jump off the left foot, right foot and both feet together. You soon learn that running and jumping off one leg will allow you to jump much higher. If you are attempting to head the ball while jumping and turning, it is best to jump with the leg that is closer to the ball. Learn also to head the ball as it comes from both the left side and the right side.

You can also practise ball control using your head by balancing the ball on your forehead. This is a fun exercise. Set yourself a target of how long you can keep the ball balanced.

Best tip. **When you are learning to head the ball, try to concentrate on accuracy to get the ball to go where you want it to.** Do not worry about power or distance – these will improve as you get older and stronger. Try to head the ball to a teammate rather than heading it aimlessly. Do not be too concerned if the ball goes to an opponent, as an attentive coach will be aware of your intentions and help you correct any recurring problem.

GOALKEEPING

11

Every young player should learn the skills of a goalkeeper. Here's why. In defence, it is very important to know what position your goalkeeper is going to take up in relation to where the ball is. Also, it can be critical to have a good idea of where the ball will rebound if the goalkeeper makes a save but does not hold on to the ball.

In attack, it is useful to understand where the hardest place is for a goalkeeper to save a shot or a header. Goalkeepers learn about positioning, angles and what it feels like to be the last person defending the goal.

Goalkeepers in the modern game have to have a high level of ball control. They must be able to have a controlled touch, in particular when the ball is played back to them by one of their own players. This is critical because the laws of the game do not permit goalkeepers to use their hands when the ball has been deliberately kicked to them by teammates.

Goalkeepers need to be able to control the ball competently with both feet, as well as with their thighs, chest and sometimes even their head!

PARENTS

While some young children may show a particular interest in goalkeeping, it is still a good idea for them to learn all the skills and techniques that are required of an outfield player. Specialised goalkeeping sessions are usually available for those players who have a keen interest in goalkeeping, and parents can help a child develop good goalkeeping skills with regular practice at home.

Goalkeeping is a particularly difficult task, both physically and mentally. If a goalkeeper makes a mistake, the probability of conceding a goal is usually high. To reassure young goalkeepers, remind them that a goalkeeper occupies a unique position in football in that they are the only player allowed to use their hands in their penalty area.

COACH

A major part of the goalkeeper's function is to make it as difficult as possible for an opponent to score a goal. One way a goalkeeper does this is by narrowing the angle between the ball and the goal that is being protected.

You can teach the players how to narrow the angle by getting them to stand with a ball a short distance away from any size of a goal *(see overleaf)*. If the goalkeeper stays on the goal line, the players will see that it is easy for them to score. However, for every step forward the goalkeeper takes, the space in the goals for attacking players to score into

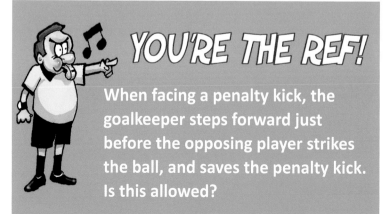

YOU'RE THE REF!

When facing a penalty kick, the goalkeeper steps forward just before the opposing player strikes the ball, and saves the penalty kick. Is this allowed?

is reduced, and it becomes much harder for them to score. Repeat this for different positions around

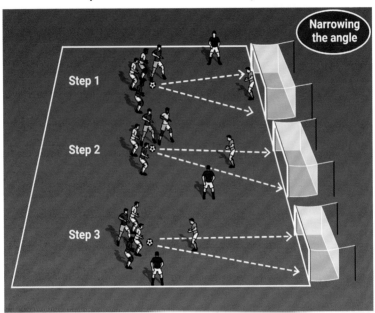

the goal and let all the players take on the role of goalkeeper. They will soon understand the principle of "narrowing the angle".

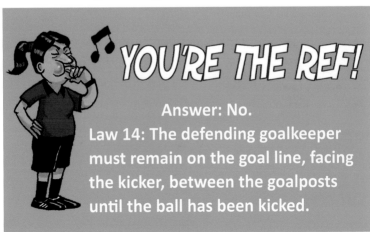

YOU'RE THE REF!

Answer: No.
Law 14: The defending goalkeeper must remain on the goal line, facing the kicker, between the goalposts until the ball has been kicked.

Playing mini-games with no goalkeepers will naturally lead to defenders looking over their shoulders to see where the goals are and adjusting their positions accordingly. This is hugely beneficial in developing positional sense.

The player nearest the goals will also be more prepared to block the ball with whatever part of their body they can, particularly if there are no other team members on hand to prevent the other team from scoring. This will lead to a much better understanding of the role of the goalkeeper and to a better defensive mind-set.

PLAYER

Like many other football techniques and skills, goalkeeping can be practised alone, especially if you have a wall or other rebound surface. Naturally, having lessons from a qualified goalkeeping coach is an essential part of the development of a superb goalkeeper. This ensures that the developing keeper can work with confidence, knowing that they are learning the correct techniques and skills.

An essential part of goalkeeping is learning to field the ball on the ground and in the air. One way to field the ball on the ground securely is to kneel on one knee, putting that leg as close as possible

to the heel of the standing foot so the ball cannot go through the legs. The goalkeeper is now ready to collect the ball and prepare to throw or pass it to a teammate. Again, as in outfield play, getting the body in line with the flight or path of the ball as soon as possible makes it easier to field the ball successfully.

Standing on the front or the balls of the feet makes it easier to move quickly to get into position to catch the ball.

For shots that are bound for the corner of the goals, it will be necessary to move the feet quickly in order to dive and make a successful save.

Staying on one's feet when making a save means that the goalkeeper will be in a better position to start a quick attack by promptly distributing the ball to an alert teammate.

YOU'RE THE REF!

A goalkeeper takes a goal kick. There is a strong wind, and the ball goes directly into the opponent's goal.
Do you award a goal?

If the ball is in the air or at chest height, the goalkeeper can catch it by forming a "W" shape behind the ball with the thumbs and index fingers. Younger goalkeepers can bring their wrists closer together to help them stop the ball.

Once the ball has been caught or is in the goalkeeper's hands, the laws of the game state that it must be released within six seconds. It is therefore a good idea to learn to run out to the edge of the penalty area and throw or pass the ball to a teammate. Remember, though, that keeping

YOU'RE THE REF!

Answer: Yes.
Law 16: A goal may be scored directly from a goal kick, but only against the opposing team.

your eye on the ball and securing it is initially much more important than thinking about how you will distribute it.

A competent coach will instruct the goalkeeper to always try to pass or throw the ball deliberately to a teammate and, whenever possible, to keep it on the ground. This makes it easier for the outfield player to control and keep possession of the ball.

The coach will also teach players to move into a position to receive the ball from their goalkeeper once the goalkeeper has possession of the ball.

Catching the ball high in the air can be a difficult skill to learn. Most of the time, a goalkeeper using outstretched arms will be able to jump and catch the ball at a much higher point than an outfield player jumping and trying to head it.

The aim, when jumping like this, is to catch the ball at the highest point of your jump, and land safely without injury and without dropping the ball. If the ball is not caught at this high point, an opponent has a much better chance of heading the ball and scoring a goal.

Good timing is critical in the jump and can best be achieved by effective coaching and regular practice. Through coaching and practice you will also learn to punch or parry the ball away from the goal when it is not possible to catch it. It is however best to become proficient at catching the ball. Goalkeepers can wear special gloves which help them do this more efficiently.

TACKLING

12

A tackle must be made in a safe and non-aggressive manner. In the modern game, tackling and defending are about positioning, anticipation, interception and making as little physical contact as possible with the opponent. Tackling is a central feature of the game, and the more frequently a team can regain possession of the ball, the better its chances to score a goal.

PARENTS

Tackling and defending are integral parts of learning the game of football. Experiencing safe tackling can help a young player get used to physical contact. They need to understand that losing possession of the ball and trying to win it back is a significant part of the game. Learning the skills associated with tackling and defending will help the player become confident, competent and happy to engage in the physical element of the game.

COACH

A good deal of defending involves running backwards – either to take up a good position to help protect the goals, or when an opponent is dribbling with the ball trying to get past a defender to cross or shoot.

Defenders must develop a high level of mental alertness and concentration and learn about good starting positions in relation to where the ball and their opponents are. Awareness, positioning and anticipation will help defenders to prevent goal scoring situations from occurring.

Exercise 1. An excellent way to teach defending and tackling in a safe, controlled and efficient manner is to start with two rows of players facing each other about two metres apart. *(See next page.)* No footballs are necessary so that the players can concentrate solely on running.

Begin with row A moving towards row B in a straight line, pretending to dribble with a football.

As row A moves forward, row B starts to run backwards. Start off slowly so that the players in row B can keep their balance. A distance of twenty metres is sufficient for the players to cover. Both rows then stop and reverse the roles back to the start.

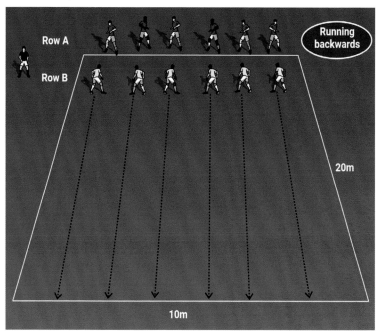

Teach the players to glance over their shoulders to check their position relative to the "attacker" and where they are going. Show them how to turn their body slightly to the side, as this will make it easier to run.

Gradually, all the players should be able to run backwards comfortably in a straight line while glancing over their shoulders. By not using a football, the players can focus on learning how to run backwards, without falling over, in a safe and controlled manner.

Using the same exercise, progress to teaching the players the correct distance they should be from the football before making the critical decision to tackle. If the defender gets too close, the opponent will easily touch the ball past them and continue the attack. However, if the defender stays too far away from the football, the opponent will have the unpressured choice of passing to a teammate or having a shot at goal.

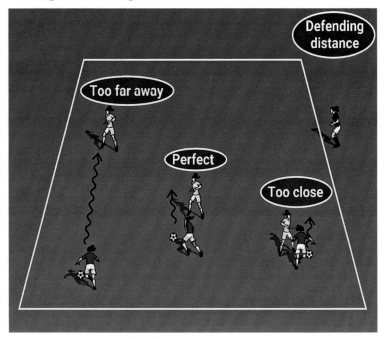

When the players understand this, they will soon work out the appropriate distance depending on the speed and skill of the opponent.

In a match situation, the defending players will also have to assess their options depending on how close they are to their goal and how many supporting players they or their opponent have.

Keeping the correct distance will put the attacker under pressure, as it is clear the defender is in a good position to make a tackle and potentially regain possession of the ball. It is also much harder for the opponent to look up and pass or shoot.

At this stage in the exercise, you can now start using footballs. Start with row A dribbling with the ball. As the defenders *(row B or yellows)* run

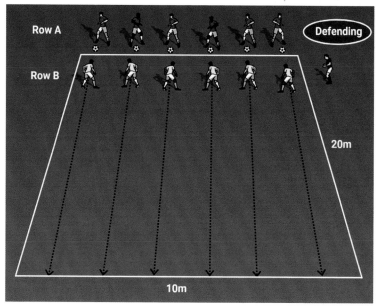

backwards, they do not tackle but instead count the number of times they potentially could have tackled and touched the ball away from their opponent.

This practice helps them learn that opponents can sometimes lose control of the ball and make it much easier for the defenders to gain possession.

Exercise 2. The next stage is to teach the defending players how to feint or pretend to commit to a tackle, in order to delay the opponent or trick them into making a mistake and losing control of the ball. The easiest trick is simply to feint to stop and tackle but carrying on running backwards. This may be sufficient for the opponent to panic and lose control of the ball.

Even if this does not work, it will usually make the attacker slow down and make it harder for them to run past the defender. It will also delay the attacker and make it easier for a teammate to catch up and help the defender to dispossess the opponent.

Finally, introduce tackling where the opponent is allowed to attempt to go past the defender, and the defender is allowed to tackle or take the ball from the opponent.

Part of the art of defending is to get the opponent to do what you want them to do. Usually, the aim is to get the opponent as far away from the goals as possible. So it is essential to know where you want the opponent to go, and to try to guide them in

that direction. It may be closer to the touchline, where there is less space for the opponent to get past with the ball, or it may be to steer them towards a teammate so that, by combining your efforts, it is possible to regain possession.

Determine the opponent's strongest or preferred foot. Sometimes, trying to force them to use their weaker foot can increase the chances of them losing control of the ball. The defender's situation is complicated because, in practice, these decisions have to be made in split seconds.

To help young players practise their new defensive skills, let them play 1v1, 2v2, 3v3, 4v4, and their variables. 1v1, for example, is just one person against another. It is one of the best exercises to practise defending or attacking, as it teaches players to make decisions on their own and to experience the different emotions associated with winning and losing the ball.

Exercise 3. In this exercise, each player has to prevent their opponent from dribbling or running

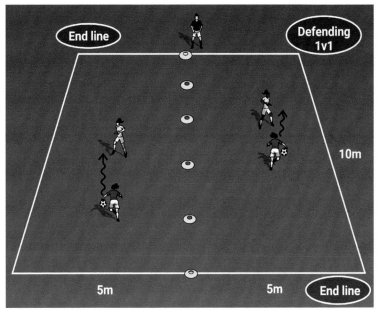

with the ball over the end line. They will soon learn what they are good at and what they need

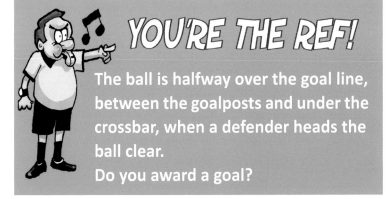

YOU'RE THE REF!

The ball is halfway over the goal line, between the goalposts and under the crossbar, when a defender heads the ball clear.
Do you award a goal?

to improve on. By changing the pairings around, everybody plays against players with different talents.

A proficient coach will encourage players to make decisions quickly and help them perfect the defensive skills they need in a 1v1 situation.

Defending in a 2v2 situation helps the players learn to communicate and cooperate with another player. *(See next page.)* Here, they have to learn to recognise each other's skills and capabilities and work together to achieve their desired outcome.

If players are defending in a 2v2 situation, not only must they be aware of their opponent but they must also take up a position to cover their teammate if he or she is beaten. As a defender in a 2v2 situation, usually one of three things will happen. If the direct opponent has the ball, then

♪ YOU'RE THE REF!

Answer: No.

Law 10: A goal is scored when the whole of the ball passes over the goal line, between the goalposts and under the crossbar, provided that no offence has been committed by the team scoring the goal.

the main options are having a shot or cross, getting past with the ball or else passing to the teammate.

Therefore, be alert to the two opponents playing a one-two or wall pass, as this is one of the best ways to beat defenders in a 2v2 situation.

In a 3v3 situation, not only do the players face the complexities involved in a 2v2, but they also have to be aware of what is known in footballing terms as "the third person running". This occurs when one of the two opponents who are not on the ball makes a run into an area hoping to receive the ball or distract the opponent. A defender marking this opponent may initially think this move is covered, as it seems impossible for the player who has possession of the ball to pass to this player. But if

the player with the ball passes to the second player, then angles and passing options suddenly change, and it may now be possible for the direct opponent to receive the ball. If this occurs, and the opponent has not been followed or tracked, then there is a good chance they will receive the ball and be in a goal scoring position.

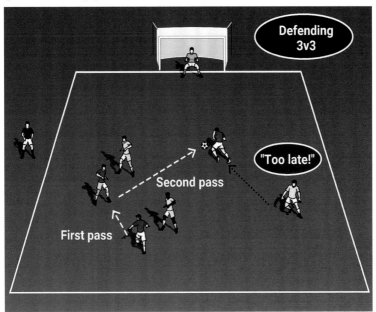

There is much to learn and many decisions to be made when defending in a 3v3 situation, so regular practice with teammates is vital.

YOU'RE THE REF!

The ball is in play when a defender starts holding an opponent outside the defender's penalty area. The defender continues to hold the opponent inside the penalty area. Do you award a penalty?

In a 4v4 situation or game, all the elements of a football match are present. The ball can be passed forwards, backwards and sideways. In this scenario,

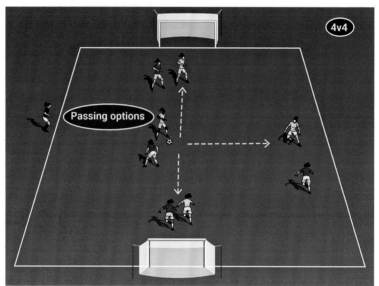

everybody defends and everybody attacks. It is a superb indicator of the fitness of the players, as they are always on the move.

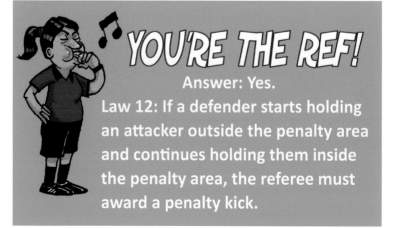

YOU'RE THE REF!

Answer: Yes.

Law 12: If a defender starts holding an attacker outside the penalty area and continues holding them inside the penalty area, the referee must award a penalty kick.

As a coach, teaching all the players how to defend 1v1, 2v2, 3v3, 4v4 and their various combinations makes it much easier to teach an entire defensive unit about starting positions, shape, organisation and communication.

Exercise 4. There are many drills and exercises to help young players learn the art of defending. The following exercise is realistic and practical, and will immediately show whether the player has learnt the basics of defending.

Player A passes the ball from inside the two-metre mark to Player B, who is inside the opposite two-metre mark. Player A then has to defend and prevent the opponent from getting the ball over Player A's end line. To do this, they should

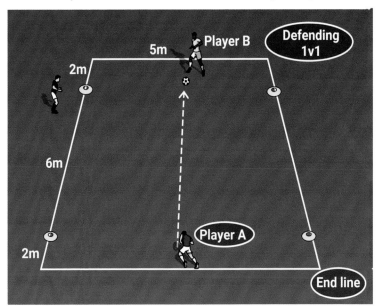

sprint towards the opponent, to the appropriate distance from Player B *(see p.124)*, and then move backwards as the opponent advances.

The aim is to force Player B to look down at the ball and then make them go to the side that Player A wants them to go to. Player A must then prepare to tackle or touch the ball out over the touchline. Player A cannot keep going back forever without making a decision, otherwise Player B will eventually get over the end line and win the challenge.

It is better for players to take decisive actions even if they turn out to be wrong. A competent coach will then help the player correct any obvious and recurring mistakes. In this exercise, it is best to concentrate on defending only and to switch the pairings often, so everyone gets to play against players of differing abilities.

This exercise is also an excellent opportunity to see how players react once they make contact with the ball. Players have to learn when it is appropriate to touch the ball out of play or clear it away from their goals, and when it is a good time to try to win possession of the ball. It is better to teach the players how to gain possession, as it is always easier to kick the ball out of play.

Keeping or regaining possession of the ball in a tackle requires good technique and skilful decision making.

A useful way to learn how to win possession of the ball is to make a "fifty-fifty tackle", where two players make contact with the ball at the same time, and both have an equal chance of gaining

control. Hit the ball in the middle, keep the ankle steady and the leg muscles tensed *(see Picture A)*. Apply firm and even pressure, and use your body strength to move the ball in the desired direction *(see Picture B)*.

YOU'RE THE REF!

A defender takes a free kick inside their own penalty area. An opponent intercepts the ball before it goes outside the penalty area, and scores.
Do you award a goal?

When teaching two players how to tackle, it is better if they are standing still, so there is less chance of either player getting hurt. They will also understand better how and where the ball moves in contact with the foot, and how the ball can then be moved to the player's advantage. It is essential to practise tackling using both the left and right foot.

Learning to defend and tackle correctly takes time and patience. The objective is to teach players to become intelligent defenders, relying more on their defensive skills and knowledge than their physical strength or size.

Tip. **Where possible, players should wear astroturf boots or moulded rubber boots, rather than studs, to help prevent any unnecessary injuries. Shin pads should also be worn.**

YOU'RE THE REF!

Answer: No.
Law 13: If, when a free kick is taken by the defending team from inside its penalty area, the ball is not kicked directly out of the penalty area, the kick is retaken.

Another kind of tackle is the sliding tackle. This is a way of stretching to reach the ball by sliding on the ground. It is often used as a last-ditch effort. If the ball is not won, however, it is much easier for the opponent to continue, as the defender is on the ground and effectively out of the game.

With this type of tackle, there is also a much higher risk of committing a foul and receiving a yellow or even a red card from the referee. A good coach will teach players to stay on their feet as long as possible, and will encourage them to use their defensive knowledge and skills to divert the opponent and the ball away from the goal.

PLAYER

Learning to defend and tackle correctly takes time and patience. Much of it is learnt in training and mini-games with friends or teammates, where there is lots of contact with the ball and opportunities to tackle and defend.

These situations enable young players to learn about positioning on the pitch in relation to the ball and fellow defenders. Errors in judgement will happen, but an attentive coach will encourage and help a young player correct any mistakes.

Players should continue to practise running backwards, looking over their shoulders and pretending that an opponent is running at them with a ball. Pass a ball against a wall and run in to close down the distance to the ball, while taking a body stance that ensures you are prepared for the next move. Remember also to practise with both feet and with different weights of pass. This will help you learn how to adopt various body positions, depending on the direction from which the ball is coming.

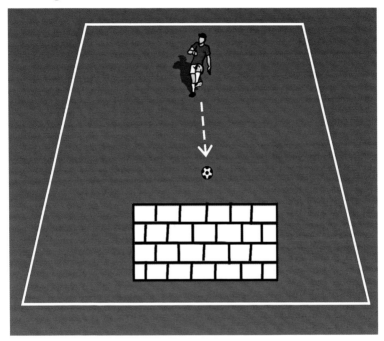

Best tip. **Do not slide or rush into tackles except as a last resort.** Stay upright for as long as possible. This will make it much harder for an opponent and easier for other defenders to come in and help out if necessary.

⓭ OUTSIDE THE BOX

"Thinking outside the box" is a cliché often used to describe new ways of thinking or being innovative and imaginative. Learning to be original at throw-ins and corner kicks can help young players stand out as intelligent footballers. Below are a few ideas which can help players become creative, confident and talented footballers.

Throw-in.

The throw-in is a method of restarting play and is an opportunity to keep or regain possession of the ball. Generally, when taking a throw-in, the aim should be to get the ball to a teammate's foot as quickly and accurately as possible. For this to happen efficiently, players continuously need to learn new ways of creating space and beating their opponents.

Throwing a ball towards a teammate's head usually makes it much harder to get the ball down on the ground and under control. There is also a much higher risk of a clash of heads.

Initially, the more quickly decisions are made, the faster you will learn what works best, and this builds up a better understanding with teammates. Remember also that you do not have to wait for the referee's whistle.

The following tips are for parents, coaches and players to learn.

Marino Branch
Brainse Marino
Tel: 8336297

1. When retrieving the ball in a mini-game or match, look around to see where teammates and opponents are positioned in relation to where you will take the throw-in.

2. Get to the ball quickly, hold it behind the head, and face the field of play at the spot where the ball went out of play.

3. Remember the laws. Keep all or part of both feet on or behind the touchline, and release the ball from behind and over the head.

4. Ideally, throw the ball to a teammate's feet.

5. Immediately step back onto the pitch once the ball is thrown in.

6. Be prepared and in a position to receive a return pass from your teammate and have an idea of what to do next with the ball.

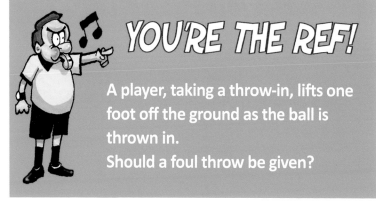

YOU'RE THE REF!

A player, taking a throw-in, lifts one foot off the ground as the ball is thrown in.
Should a foul throw be given?

Below is a simple exercise that will help the players become effective at taking throw-ins. After receiving the ball from the thrower, the attacker and

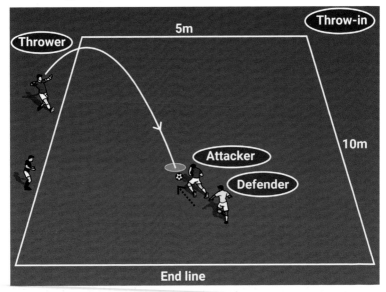

the thrower must try to manoeuvre the ball past the defender in a 2v1 situation and run or dribble with the ball over the end line.

🎵 **YOU'RE THE REF!**

Answer: No.
Law 15: A goal cannot be scored directly from a throw-in. In this case, as the ball has entered the thrower's goal, a corner kick is awarded to the opposition.

PLAYER

Practise throw-ins alone by simply throwing a ball against a wall or other rebound surface from various distances, and experience the different angles and speeds at which the ball comes back. Visualise where the target for the throw-in is, to

improve accuracy, or put a few small marks on the wall as targets. Practise stepping up to an imaginary line (or a piece of string or similar) on the ground, taking the throw-in, then stepping onto the playing area immediately and controlling the ball.

Initial mistakes resulting in a foul throw tend to be as a consequence of lifting one foot off the ground or having one or two feet over the touchline.

Practise controlling the ball once it comes back from the rebound surface. Practise feints that are designed to lose a marker, and try getting to the bounce of the ball to have options on how to control or pass it. Also, work on shielding the ball from an imaginary opponent.

Corner kick. Because of the distance between the corner of the field of play and the goal, it is usually a player with a strong kick who takes a corner kick. While there may be more than one person on a team who can do this, there will inevitably be players who miss out on learning the skills associated with taking a corner kick.

All too often we see a player kicking the ball from a corner in the general direction of the goal, hoping that one of their teammates will be able to divert the ball into the goal. Eventually, this team will encounter a skilled goalkeeper who will be well coached and able to catch these types of crosses.

They will also play against tall defenders who will simply head the ball away from the goal.

Players should be taught to view corners as an exciting chance to create goal scoring opportunities, no matter how tall, strong or talented their opponents might be. Under these circumstances,

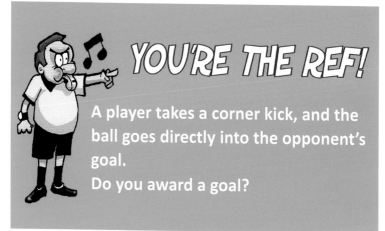

they will be motivated to learn the skills more quickly and to understand the reasons for doing so.

PARENTS

Helping your child to practise 1v1 and 2v1 at home is extremely beneficial, as these situations occur quite often in a short corner routine. Developing players must be encouraged continually because not all short corner routines are successful. Perseverance is the key, and the skills learnt will also help the players in their general outfield play.

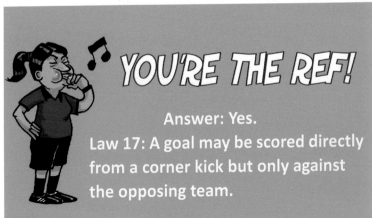

YOU'RE THE REF!

Answer: Yes.

Law 17: A goal may be scored directly from a corner kick but only against the opposing team.

COACH

Teach the players the laws of the game in relation to a corner kick. The fact that their opponents must stand 10 yards or 9.15 metres away gives the advantage to the attacking team.

Short corners or quick corners typically involve two or more players. In many situations, a 2v1 will occur. *(See step one below.)* It is therefore essential to teach the players how to use the space and make good passing and receiving angles in order to get

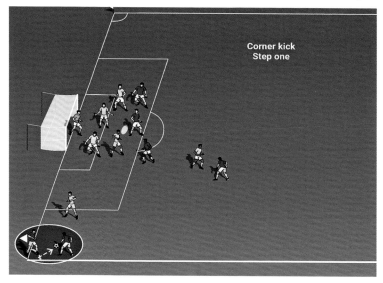

Corner kick
Step one

past the opponent quickly and move closer towards the goal.

When the players are retrieving the ball to take the corner, teach them to look around to see where their teammates and opponents are positioned. Instruct them to get to the ball quickly, place the ball inside the corner arc and make their decision.

The closer they get to the goal with the ball, the more the opposition will be forced to come out to tackle them. This will leave more space in the goal area *(see step two below),* thus increasing the chances of a goal being the outcome.

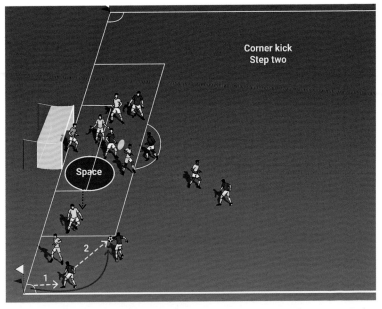

Corner kick
Step two

Space

2

1

Most short corner routines involve quick, accurate passing with some individual skill, and it is this type of practice that the players relish.

There are many player combinations that can be used in short corner routines, and the more that players practise, the more they will succeed.

If the opposition is not prepared for a corner, and if the player taking the corner kick can pass the ball a longer distance, then they should be encouraged to take the corner quickly, as it increases the chances of an unmarked teammate having a free shot at goal.

In the routine below, a quick pass to the front or near post area directed at an unmarked teammate can catch the opposition unprepared. Not all short

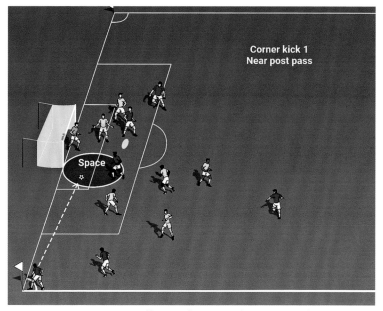

Corner kick 1
Near post pass

Space

corner routines will work out the way they were intended. However, a good coach will encourage the players to persevere and help them improve.

The laws of the game state that the referee's whistle is not needed to restart play from a throw-in, a corner kick, a dropped ball, a goal kick or most free kicks. Therefore, at a corner kick, a quick-thinking player can gain an advantage. Players should practise from both sides of the pitch.

Another routine is a quick pass to a teammate at the edge of the penalty area. This gives the teammate the opportunity of a shot or a more accurate cross.

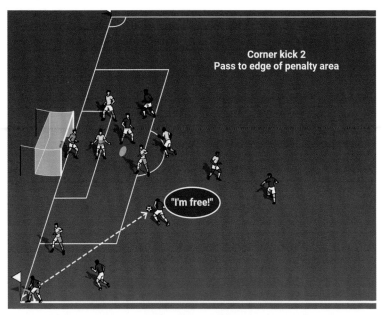

Corner kick 2
Pass to edge of penalty area

"I'm free!"

It is important to take advantage of the law that your opponent must stand 10 yards or 9.15 metres away until the ball is in play from a corner kick. However, you do not have to wait for this to happen.

PLAYER

The main skills involved in short corners are short accurate passing, making correct angles to pass and receive the ball, and using a 2v1 situation to beat an opponent. To perfect these skills, practise the following corner kick routine with a few friends, and remember to practise from both sides of the football pitch.

YOU'RE THE REF!

A player removes the corner flagpost before they take a corner kick.
Do you allow play to continue?

In the routine below, once player 1 has kicked the ball into play by passing to player 2, she should run around the back of player 2, not in front of her. In

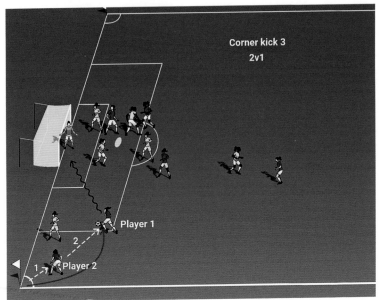

doing so, she will not impede her teammate and allow their opponent to make a tackle and take the ball from them. Player 1 should now be able to

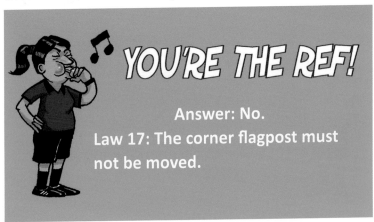

run on to the return pass and be in a much better position to shoot at goal or make a more accurate cross towards her teammates.

Quick thinking and brave decision making are important, and regular practising of short corner routines will lead to making the most out of corner kicks. It will be much easier if the rest of your teammates are alert and committed to this style of creative play. Look for opportunities in open play to catch an opponent unawares, and you will become a more creative and intelligent footballer.

PROPER PREPARATION

PARENTS

Getting children into a routine for training and matches helps to build confidence, as they will know in advance where they are going and what they will be doing. Simple things like showing a youngster how to pack a kitbag will help them on the pathway to developing independence and confidence.

It is vital for players to arrive at the training session warm and ready to get started. If the weather is cold or wet, the player should wear a warm training top, possibly a waterproof top, and leggings, hat and gloves.

Once the training session commences, it is much easier to take clothing off if the weather improves. In this way, valuable time is not wasted having to warm players up to avoid injury before they are ready to play football.

Wearing astroturf boots on the way to training is safer than studded boots, and if the players train on an artificial surface, then they are ready to go. If they play or practise on grass, then simply put on moulded or studded boots. An attentive coach will always check that players are adequately prepared for the conditions. With time and experience, the players will learn to be prepared and ready for all situations and eventualities.

In wet conditions, a useful tip is to have a towel in the kitbag for the player to dry off at any stage. A strong plastic bag into which the kitbag can be placed is also useful, as it can prevent the bag and its contents from getting soaked. It is always wise to have a change of boots in the kitbag.

It is also useful to learn basic first aid. The vast majority of injuries are knocks and bruises to the lower limbs, and if treated promptly they can pretty much be eliminated as a reason to miss training.

If you are planning to go to watch your child playing or training, bring a first aid kit and a cool bag with a cold flexible pack or instant disposable cold packs. Do not rely on somebody else. The sooner an injury is treated, the shorter the recovery time will be.

The **PRICER** acronym points to an efficient methodology for treating knocks and bruises.

Protection

Rest

Ice

Compression

Elevation

Rehabilitation

An ice pack or a cold pack is a key component in the treatment of soft-tissue injuries. Early application is essential, and the more muscular an area is, the longer the time that ice can usually be applied. The quicker the injury is treated, the faster it should heal, and normal movement of the injured limb should be encouraged as soon as possible. Consultation with a physiotherapist will involve discussing the optimal loading of the injured tissue – you will get advice on when to move, stretch and strengthen and by how much.

COACH

Preparing well for a coaching session will result in a more productive, enjoyable and rewarding time for all. Arriving early is not always possible, but it allows time to plan and organise, particularly if circumstances change at the last minute.

It is therefore helpful to have the assistance of a parent who is normally there in a supporting

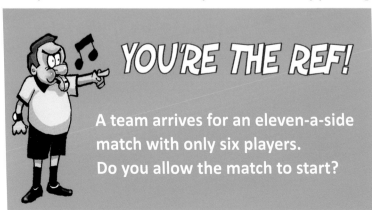

YOU'RE THE REF!

A team arrives for an eleven-a-side match with only six players. Do you allow the match to start?

capacity but who can stand in if requested. Support assistants should have a duplicate set of training equipment (and, if possible, a brief outline of the session) so that the entire training or coaching session is not dependent on the coach always being present. Having a support assistant is also important from a health and safety viewpoint.

Punctuality benefits everybody, and starting on time is a fine example to set for the players. Players arriving promptly and suitably attired means there is less time spent warming up and much more time with the football. It is usually much easier to work with cones and bibs, as they help with setting boundaries and with making changes more quickly and with less explanation.

If the players come equipped with their water bottles, it is simple to allow them to take a quick

YOU'RE THE REF!

Answer: No.
Law 3: A match may not start or continue if either team has fewer than seven players.

drink at various intervals before moving on to the next part in the coaching session. This also helps to pass more responsibility to the players regarding hydration.

It is also part of the role of the coach to teach the players to be responsible with the footballs, particularly if they all have one each and are eager to get started! A child being struck and hurt by a stray football is not how anyone wants a coaching session to start or end. One way to avoid this is to begin immediately with a pre-planned warm-up. By instilling good discipline and manners, you reduce dramatically the chance of a child getting hurt while under your supervision.

The following is an abbreviated example of a one-hour coaching session played in a safe and organised environment. The players should arrive five minutes early and properly prepared.

1. Warm up with a football each. Dribbling in a confined area, one step per touch, head up, left foot, right foot, outside of the foot, inside of the foot, stop with the right foot, and stop with the left foot. Add skills.
2. Passing with both feet, static and then while the players are moving. Keep the distance short (five to ten metres), head up, eye contact.
3. Control of the ball on the ground and in the air with both feet, thigh, chest and (if appropriate) the head. Static practice and then while the players are moving.
4. Demonstration and practice of one coaching topic for approximately fifteen minutes. Try to have all the players active with a ball.
5. Mini-games focusing on the coaching topic, and then free play for approximately twenty minutes.
6. Cool down and a quick chat.

Note: Points 1–3 can all be combined but should be the basic building block of each session and should last for approximately twenty minutes of the one-hour session. For younger players, point 4 can be carried out immediately after the warm-up. Always assess the players under your supervision and be prepared to be flexible.

Tips for a game.
1. Make pitch size appropriate to the number of players and the topic being taught.
2. Encourage the use of short and quick corner kicks in mini-games.
3. Encourage quick throw-ins and free kicks to help the players make prompt decisions.
4. No need for goalkeepers. All players attack and defend and do not use their hands.
5. Award two goals when a player deliberately shoots into the bottom corner of a goal.

YOU'RE THE REF!

You need to re-start a game with a drop ball. However, one of the players kicks the ball before it touches the ground.
Do you allow the game to continue?

🟤 GETTING IN TIP-TOP SHAPE

Football is an excellent sport for general fitness. It involves walking, jogging, running, sprinting and jumping.

Looking after one's health, preparing properly, preventing unnecessary injuries and using skills and ideas from other sports and games will help the young player to become the best footballer they can be.

Sport is a great way to help children develop a healthy relationship with food and drinks, as they will soon take an interest in learning which ones are healthy and of benefit to them in their particular sport.

If we encourage children to exercise, then we must help them learn about proper nutrition and healthy living. Children need to eat energy-rich foods. Complex or good carbohydrates release glucose slowly into the bloodstream and help keep energy levels consistent. Examples of these are brown rice, potatoes, wholegrain bread, porridge, nuts, fruit and vegetables. Refined or bad carbohydrates are the opposite, as they release glucose quickly, resulting in erratic energy levels. Some examples are white bread, chocolate, sweets, jams and soft drinks.

Children also need protein, such as chicken and fish, which is crucial to their growth and development. Whenever possible, protein should be included in their meals, especially after training and matches, as protein is essential in helping recovery as well as muscle repair. Good fats such as fish, meat, olive oil, nuts and seeds are good for the brain as well as overall health. Bad fats such as crisps, processed foods and fried foods should generally be avoided.

The best liquid to drink is water, but milk is beneficial immediately after a match or training. The human body depends on water, so insufficient water will lead to dehydration, which will drain energy and severely reduce performance.

When to eat and drink is also important. Eating approximately three hours before training or matches gives the body time to digest.

Water should be sipped in the few hours before training or a match. A great way to encourage a child to drink enough liquid is to provide them with their own water bottle which they can bring with them. If they sip the water before training and matches, they will avoid possible dehydration, and their strength and stamina will improve.

Tips. **The best time to refuel is immediately after training or a match.** Good posture and flexibility can help the youngster become a superb athlete.

Breathing in and out through the nose, rather than the mouth, can help improve your health as well as sleep patterns and concentration levels. Looking after teeth and gums from an early age is also very important. Hopefully, the players will learn quickly, enjoy the game of football and achieve their full potential.

A FINAL FOCUS

There are other sports and games which can benefit an all-round footballer. Swimming can be of immense value to children, as they can learn to float and swim within a year of being born. They develop confidence, balance, coordination and muscle strength and a love for a sport that can potentially save their life.

Cross-country running is good for building stamina, and orienteering is great for general fitness, spatial awareness and decision making.

Chess is another game which stimulates the brain and has similarities to football. Some players (or in chess, pieces) have different capabilities from others, and some work better in various combinations. Both sides have an end goal in mind and usually a time limit in which to achieve it. In both football and chess, there is the need to plan ahead and try to outwit an opponent. In both games, there are also pre-rehearsed moves to use at different stages of the game.

Mental visualisation is valuable in learning to play football. Seeing the activity taking place in the mind can help with physically carrying it out. Mentally breaking a skill or technique down into its parts and rebuilding it can help the brain make the necessary connections and decisions that are required to carry it out physically.

There is absolutely nothing wrong with thinking and dreaming of scoring fantastic goals, making great saves or tackles. This can benefit the young footballer and add to their overall enjoyment of the game.

Football can also help children in their academic career. Learning a skill and then seeing how they can use it on a football pitch can help them in learning other subjects. Once something is understood and can be associated with a physical action or an experience, it is then much easier to keep it in the memory.

Respect and good manners are important in football. Respect for the referee, opponents, teammates, family and friends will help develop a real enjoyment of the game of football. Many players have played their entire careers without having been sent off the field of play, and having a positive and friendly attitude can help developing players to achieve their goals.

Since the laws of the game are the same the world over, it is also possible to learn some words in a different language. For example, in football when you put a ball through an opponent's legs, it is usually called a nutmeg in English. In the French language, it is called "petit pont", which means little bridge. The shape of a little rounded bridge ∩ makes it easy to understand how it can be compared to the shape of a player's legs.

Probably the hardest law to learn in football is the offside law. The simplest way to learn this law is to remember that there must be at least two opponents between the player and the opponent's goal line when the ball is played to the player. A player cannot be offside:

- in their own half of the pitch;

- if they are behind the ball;

- if they are level with the second-last opponent or the last two opponents;

- if they receive the ball directly from a throw-in, corner kick or goal kick.

There are examples to help explain the offside law in *Laws of the Game,* published by the International Football Association Board. For a copy of the laws in booklet form, contact your national football association or visit the FIFA website at www.fifa.com.

Progressing into eleven-a-side football will be much easier if a player is confident, competent, determined and enthusiastic and has an inquisitive mind. It is also a great benefit if the player has an excellent coach and is encouraged by parents.

I hope this book has provided the information and a little inspiration so that the next stages of learning in a young footballer's career will be as enjoyable and rewarding as the formative years.

Keith Gillespie, Tommy Wright, Brian Strain, Mark Langhammer, Niall Stacey, Michael Willis, Tim Dalton, Nigel Best, Ian Stewart, Alfie Wylie, Roger Anderson, Stephen Hamilton, Alan Cairns, Tom Stark, Morag Stark, Damian O'Beirne, Niall O'Regan, Shane McCullough, Jim Lawlor, Jim Gracey, Phillip Toy, Seamus Heath, Phil Abbott, Aaron Callaghan, James Hilliard, John Laverty, Joe McAree, Robert Casey, Neil Coleman, Colin Malone, JP Kelly, James Dooley, Tony Kavanagh, Adrian Beattie, Cameron Ramsey, Dan Brown, Paul Evans and Tony McCall.

Particular thanks are extended to Dave Ager, not only for writing the foreword but for his advice and sharing his experience of years of official involvement in the game of football.

Thanks also to Stan Carey for his copy-editing, proofreading and advice on this book.

Thanks are extended to Jacques, Lili Rose and Ciarán for their patience and their modelling skills! Finally, I would like to thank my family and friends, some of whom are no longer with us, for their help and support during my football career.

Trevor McMullan

INDEX

Page numbers in **bold** refer to the *You're The Ref!* sections.